Special Operations Mindset

Develop the Champion Mindset of the Best-Trained & Most Elite Forces in the World

Copyright © 2021 by Littlestone

All rights reserved. No part of this publication may be reproduced, distributed or transmitted in any form or by any means, without prior written permission.

Special Operations Mindset
Paperback - 1st ed.
ISBN: 978-1-946373-11-3
$17.99 everywhere great books are sold

Contents

Intro 5
1: Training (PTREXAR) 14
2: Truth 19
3: Competence 32
4: Confidence 47
5: Discipline 69
6: Commitment 83
7: Motivation 103
8: Responsibility 127
9: Courage 148
10: Intensity 163
11: Mental Toughness 178
12: Industriousness 203
13: Readiness 223
Conclusion 248

Intro

What makes a Special Forces "Green Beret" jump out of an airplane in the dark, at night, with all his gear, only to land and then begin the real mission?

What makes an Air Force Pararescueman get back into the swimming pool, ten minutes after being pulled out unconscious?

What motivates a Marine Raider to carry a hundred-pound rucksack all day long?

What makes a Ranger go days without sleep, and yet he is still as dependable and as capable as if he arrived fresh?

What makes a Navy SEAL give his life for his country? Team? Buddies?

The answer is complicated—but the people who do these kinds of heroic activities aren't. They are simply the best. Some say Special Operators are the best because they train and develop their skills and competencies. Others say they are the best because they were born aggressive, self-reliant, committed, focused. I say it is a bit of both … nature and nurture.

Greetings, my name is Christopher Littlestone and I have had the unique honor of serving with some of the most amazing and capable men and women in the world. As the creator behind the "Life is a Special Operation" YouTube channel, I have spent the last several years since my Army retirement trying to inspire, educate, and strengthen the next generation of leaders. I can't tell you how many times a week I get asked about developing a winner's mindset or how to build Mental Toughness. It seems like everyone is in search of a secret recipe that is going to take their performance to the next level. But there isn't a secret recipe. Unless you call deliberate study and hard work a secret.

In case you are new to "Life is a Special Operation," let me quickly summarize what makes my perspective and experience so unique and why I am qualified to write about the Special Operations Mindset. Since I can remember, I always wanted to be an officer in the Army. I wanted to be an amazing leader who would change the world. Of course, I was a bit naïve back then, but it helped keep me focused on developing the skills required to be successful in the military. I took martial arts and was the captain of the chess club and cross-country team. I was on the swim team, debate team, an Eagle Scout, and like most industrious young men whose parents want them to learn self-sufficiency early in life, I worked from the week I turned sixteen until the week I reported in to an all-men's military university, where I graduated with academic stars, a cadet captain, and a member of the Honor committee. Because I wanting to fly MEDEVAC helicopters, I requested and got a commission into the Medical Service Corps. Despite applying three years in a row, I was never "picked up" for pilot training. But during those years, I was a HMMWV Ambulance Platoon Leader in Korea, a Medical Platoon Leader in the 2/502 Infantry at Fort Campbell, and the Company Commander of a small hospital in Honduras. I realized that besides two years of Battalion Command, I was destined to spend the next fifteen years of my life as a staff officer. Looking for alternatives, Special Forces was plan "A," becoming a physician's assistant or attending medical school was plan "B." Staying in the Medical Service Corps was plan "C." Thankfully I was well-prepared, and plan "A" was a success. I've never looked back.

The next forty-eight months blended into a whirlwind of training and development. Special Forces Assessment and Selection (SFAS) was followed by six months at Fort Benning, Georgia for the Infantry Captain's Career Course (IC3). I then spent six weeks at Fort Leavenworth for the Combines Arms Service Staff School (CAS3) before reporting in to Fort Bragg for the Special Forces Qualification Course (Q Course) and Survival, Evasion, Resistance, & Escape (SERE) school. After graduation from the Q Course, I went to Ranger school, Dive school and the Special Operations Tactical Air Control (SOTAC) course.

Within days of arriving to my Special Forces Operational Detachment Alpha (ODA), I was back in the field, taking what I learned in the schoolhouse to the next level. The "Dive team" I had the privilege of commanding was comprised of some of the brightest, toughest, and most intense men who have ever put on uniform. As in all Special Operations units, if we weren't deployed, we were training for the next deployment like our lives depended on it. I went to school to learn how to steal cars, race cars, crash cars. I went to Jumpmaster school, and schools that teach you how to escape when you are kidnapped. You name it, we did it.

Over the next few years, I had the privilege of serving at the front lines of freedom in the war against drugs and the global war on terror ... two months in Panama, six months in Colombia, six months in Paraguay, three months in Afghanistan, ten months in Afghanistan, six months in Afghanistan, six months in Honduras ... and then I finished off my service with three years in Belgium at the NATO Special Operations Headquarters, and two years in Germany at Special Operations Command–Europe.

As a young Major, I also had the amazing opportunity to get a Master's of Public Administration (MPA) at Harvard. I'll never forget the day I got the good news that I was accepted. My old SCUBA team had a mission to kill / capture a senior Taliban bad guy in the Helmand province of Southern Afghanistan. I was part of the "Quick Reaction Force" and helicopter "Squirter Patrol." The mission of Squirter Patrol was to chase down and capture or question military-aged males who "fled the scene of the crime." Since we were in the middle of nowhere, men trying to "squirt" or run away from the objective compound were easily chased down by two Blackhawk helicopters working in tandem, and armed with guys like me hanging out of the window with precision rifles. The mission was textbook perfect. One Taliban was killed, some intel was gathered, and a couple of squirters were deemed not to be of interest and were allowed to go. The temperature was amazing, the sky glorious, my team was strong and happy and doing what they do best, and I was as happy as a soldier could be when I returned to base and popped open my Army email.

"Congratulations, Christopher. You've been admitted to Harvard's School of Government."

Two days later, I was on a plane back to Fort Bragg. I out-processed in a record-winning three days, and I left Saturday morning with a U-Haul full of furniture and my Harley for a drive up Interstate 95 all the way to Massachusetts. Sunday night, I slept in the truck. By lunch on Monday morning, I had moved into my grad school apartment. And summer school started Tuesday morning. It was hard to believe that nine days earlier I had been in Afghanistan. I bet I was the happiest student in the world.

I tell you this background info to help you better understand who I am and where I've been. Although I always tried to be a "Quiet Professional," in my older years I have become much more humble and less inclined to talk about myself. Had my wife, some friends, and my content editor not insisted that I give you a little more history and background, I would have been content to stay anonymous in the background.

But the truth is, "it's not about me." You will notice that I'm not the hero of any of these stories. This book is about inspiring the next generation of leaders. You won't find page and page about how awesome I am, how thick my hair is, and how chiseled my abs are. I usually learn something the hard way or through being thrown into the fire. But I will gladly boast about the exceptional men with whom I have had the honor of serving.

For the most part, I organized this book into one chapter per mindset. And for each chapter we have an:

- Introduction and / or a Story
- Definition & Considerations of the Mindset
- What it is
- What it isn't
- Best Indicators Of
- Too Much or Too Little
- Implications Of
- How It's Built
- A Military, Business, and Social Example or Illustration
- And an Individual Training / Development Plan: (PTREXAR)

Classification: All stories and illustrations in this book, as far as you are concerned, are made up. Names or details within the stories have been changed to protect the privacy of my colleagues and the sensitive nature of our training methods or tactics.

No Fluff: If you know my previous works and educational videos on YouTube, you will recognize my no-fluff style. This book captures the virtues, principles, and mindset of the elite Special Operations community. It doesn't tell pages and pages of feel-good stories. I have written this book to correspond with the way I learn. I don't need a 350-page book of feel-good stories to learn the seven habits of highly effective people. I need seven sentences to tell me what they are. I'm smart enough to figure the rest out and think you are, too. The fluff simply slows me down. Feel-good books sell millions of copies to people who want to feel good. I don't want you to feel good, I want you to <u>be</u> good. My goal is nothing short of helping you to develop within yourself those characteristics which will ensure you're successful in whatever you do.

I like to highlight and underline key phrases and ideas within the books I read. This makes it easier when I want to reread a book or revisit some of its best ideas. I took the liberty of highlighting and underlying key ideas to make it easier for you to read and internalize.

Throughout this book we are going to frequently use the acronym SOF (Special Operations

Forces). Get used to me saying "SOF are the …" or, "You will never see SOF doing this or that."

All mindsets are going to be Capitalized throughout the book to add emphasis.

The point of having this mindset is partially to be a better athlete, manager, student, parent, warrior, or leader … but the mindset also should be your goal out of self-respect. You deserve to be the best you that you have the potential to be.

Whether you are an aspiring member of the Special Operations community or simply a young man or woman who is looking to develop the unstoppable mindset of a champion, we can all benefit from studying what makes the elite members of the Special Operations community so unique and successful.

Life is a Special Operation:
Are you ready for it?

1: Training (PTREXAR)

We are going to discuss "training" before we dive into Special Operations Mindsets because we need to establish our philosophical foundation. And this foundation is built upon deliberate and purposeful training.

I believe in nature and nurture. SOF guys aren't born stronger, tougher, and more capable than anyone else. They develop their skills and mindset over time … through training … through overcoming challenges … through failures … and through success. You don't just wake up as a Special Operations Soldier. You go through years of training to hone and sharpen your skills. If there is only one thing that you take away from this book, it should be the fact that <u>Special Operations Forces train harder than anyone else</u>. They give 100%, day in, day out, because they know that the harder they train, the more prepared they will be. And this is why Training is the first mindset.

Special Operations Training model: **PTREXAR**

P: Plan

    T: Train

        R: Rehearse

            EX: Execute

                A: Analyze

                    R: Repeat.

Let's illustrate how PTREXAR works, using shooting skills as an example.

<u>Plan:</u> Your Special Operations team is deploying, and you want to make sure that everyone is shooting well and that all of their optics and scopes are perfectly "zeroed." You make a plan to spend a week at the range and then do an overnight training mission. You plan and request training ranges, training facilities, ammunition, medical safety support, and everything you need for a final training mission.

<u>Train:</u> You spend days at the range, shooting your rifles and pistols until your fingers are chapped and calloused from loading and reloading ammunition into your magazines. Then you shoot at night, in the dark, with flashlights. Then you shoot at night, in the dark, with infrared lights and lasers and night-vision goggles. Then

you do collective training with the other members of your team. Then you add in variations and different types of scenarios.

<u>Rehearse</u>: You are now ready to do rehearsals. You invent a scenario, rearrange the targets at the range, and then attack it using different techniques and methods. You do your first rehearsal in daylight. Then you do a rehearsal mission at night.

<u>Execute</u>: Now you want to put all your training together during a fully supported and resourced training mission. Your team plans the mission, conducts a parachute infiltration, patrols (hikes) to the objective, conducts reconnaissance and observes the objective, attacks the objective, shoots the bad guys, rescues the hostage, and then moves to the designated helicopter landing zone, where you all get picked up by the helicopters that bring you back to headquarters for medical treatment and a debrief.

<u>Analyze</u>: Your team conducts an After-Action Report (AAR) to discuss Lessons Learned (LL). You discuss what you did right to incorporate these practices into your team's Standard Operating Procedures (SOPs). But more importantly, you focus on what went wrong and / or what you can improve.

Repeat: Despite finishing one training iteration, you don't rest on your laurels. You don't kick up your feet and relax. You repeat the entire training process to take your individual skills and team's collective abilities to the next level.

PTREXAR is an effective tool to use for anything that can be trained. Whether we are learning how to shoot weapons, as illustrated above, or practicing how to assemble and operate a zodiac boat in the dark, **PTREXAR** will help you systematically improve and perfect any skill ... or mindset.

Frequently, you will not need to focus on all points of PTREXAR. For example, you want to make sure that everyone on your team is able to set up and use an encrypted, Top-Secret communication device. You don't need a huge Plan, and likely you don't need to Analyze how to make the training better. You simply need to pull out the radio and practice using it (Train, Execute), over and over again (Repeat), until it becomes second nature. Then, do it in the office with the lights off using your red flashlight (Rehearse).

The rest of the book discusses the top mindsets that I've observed in the Special Operations Forces with whom I have had the honor of working. You might have some of the mindsets already. For sure, you will recognize them and understand them. The key is to adopt them and use them to make your world better. And that takes a deliberate approach ... **PTREXAR**.

For example, if you want to develop Competence, then attack it using **PTREXAR**. <u>Plan</u> for Competence. <u>Train</u> for Competence. <u>Rehearse</u> Competence. <u>Execute</u> Competence. <u>Analyze</u> your successes and shortcomings. Then <u>Repeat</u>. This is how you will train, develop, and own Special Operations Mindsets. Be vigilant. Never stop training and developing your skills and mindset.

2: Truth

We can't study the mindset that makes Special Operations Forces so successful without discussing honesty. For the most part, we all know what is true and what isn't true. <u>The bigger problem is that people lie to themselves and believe what they want to believe, or they only surround themselves with those who tell them what they want to hear, regardless of whether or not it corresponds to reality.</u> One of the biggest flaws of our culture and the twenty-first century is that people are too scared or too weak to say the Truth. It is easier to lie and tell people what they want to hear than to tell the Truth. But it is impossible to build anything substantial, to include an elite mindset, upon lies.

Let me give a few quick examples.

Chess: A friend of the family is a loving mother who tells her nine-year-old son that he is the best chess player in the world because he beats all the adults in the family. During a recent visit, I beat her son at chess, three games in a row. Mom gets upset and says I should lose. Absolutely not. I was nice and loving and had a great time playing chess with the very smart boy. But the fact is a nine-year-old will never get better at chess (or LIFE) if everyone lets him win on purpose.

Swimming: I was at the public swimming pool with a recent high school graduate who came along to do a swim workout. I asked him how good of a swimmer he was, so as to judge how hard or easy I should make our swim.

He proudly told me, "My Aunt Lisa was on a swim team for years, and she said I'm the best swimmer she has ever seen."

"Great," I thought, "he's a good swimmer." After less than thirty seconds in the pool, I realized that Aunt Lisa was not telling the Truth. This young man was a terrible swimmer. In fact, my wife, who was swimming "Glamour Laps" (breast stroke while wearing sunglasses, without getting her hair wet) lapped him twice in 500 meters.

Your mom loves you and doesn't want to hurt your feelings. But <u>if everyone in life lets you win, then you are destined to be a loser.</u> Your Confidence (in chess or LIFE) must be legitimate, not ridiculous. Your Aunt Lisa thinks she is being loving to you when she says that you are the best swimmer she has ever seen. But the Truth is, false Confidence in your swimming abilities could get you killed.

No one has to be the best at everything. You will always have weaknesses. This is normal. The key isn't to lie to yourself about your abilities. The key is to be honest with yourself. Let your Confidence be based upon Truth and reality. Let your Confidence be legitimate.

Imagine that you go to your doctor's office to get a physical checkup, or to get cleared for a mission, or to get some treatment for a medical issue. But you don't tell the doctor the Truth about your medical issue. Let's say your motives are pure. You aren't trying to deceive your doctor. You are just embarrassed. There is no way that the doctor is going to help you get well if he doesn't know what is wrong with you. Let's look at this example from the other perspective.

Would you want your doctor to tell you what you want to hear, or would you want your doctor to tell you the Truth? The answer is easy. We want our doctors to tell us the Truth. Imagine a doctor who lies. "You are not fat at all." "I don't think your high blood pressure has anything to do with your diet." Imagine your doctor saying, "Everyone survives blood cancer. You will be just fine." No. This is unacceptable. We need and we deserve the Truth.

With that said, there are nicer ways to express the Truth than to simply and mercilessly announce "You are fat," or "This cancer is for sure going to kill you, dead." This is where I encourage you to be assertive and tactful, dare I say loving. But always truthful. Nonetheless, this book is about the Special Operations Mindset, not about how to be a loving communicator … so let's get back on task.

Special Operations are a matter of life and death. There is no time for exaggeration. No time for deception. The message given must be the message received. And the message given better be the Truth.

Definition & Considerations

Truth is defined as "the quality or state of being based on fact."[1]

It is a sad commentary on modern times that I need to include a definition of the Truth. Yet, I have to. We are so surrounded by lies and deception and politically correct people who only tell people what they want to hear. We have "fake news." We have fake "professionals" who give commentary on this fake news. We have moms who tell us that we are great at chess and aunts who tell us that we are the best swimmers in the world.

---

[1] https://www.oxfordlearnersdictionaries.com/definition/english/truth

It is disgusting to see how we are surrounded by liars. "This car is safe and mechanically sound." "Do this workout, and in seven minutes you will have six-pack abs." "Do this to get rich." "Buy this to be happy." What a rip-off. And sadly, it is so prevalent that we are no longer upset when we recognize dishonesty.

What it is

<u>Truth is that which corresponds to reality</u>, to fact. You can say that the sky is green. But the Truth is that when you look up, you see blue. You can say, "I'm the strongest." But if you can't pass the minimums on the fitness test, then you obviously aren't the strongest.

What it isn't

Truth is <u>not that which corresponds to what we want or hope,</u> or what others tell us. You may want to be a world-class runner. But that doesn't make you fast or give you endurance. You may hope to be a Navy SEAL. But that doesn't mean you are one. Your friends may tell you that you look great. But that doesn't mean that you don't have fifty extra pounds of body fat.

Best Indicators of Truth

- Your friends and family disagree with you every once and a while. If they disagree with you, then they are likely not always telling you what you want to hear. If they never disagree with you, then they are likely only telling you what you want to hear.
- Hearing or seeing or learning something hurts your feelings or makes you defensive.
- Something is quantifiable and verifiable.

Yes Men

We have all heard of "Yes Men." These are friends, family members, and employees who only tell you what you want to hear. They avoid conflict by always agreeing. They don't speak the Truth. They only speak what it takes to allow them to continue living peacefully. They worship the status quo and live in a constant state for fear. They are weak humans. Don't befriend them. Don't become one. And if they are family and you are required to be near them, then set boundaries and don't adopt their weakness.

No Men

On the opposite side of the spectrum, we have "No Men." These are the guys who love conflict. They don't value the Truth. They value being right. Their highest feeling is when they can make you look bad or point out that you are mistaken. But even when you are right, they will never admit it. Avoid these types of people, and for sure don't become one. They are toxic.

Too Much or Too Little

Too much Truth, and you become the jerk that no one likes. If this is you, keep telling the Truth, but I would recommend practicing a bit of tact and assertiveness.

Too little Truth, and your perceptions are not based upon reality or fact. If this is you, then I recommend looking at the hard facts and finding new friends who love you enough to tell you the Truth.

Implications

If you have the principle of Truth engrained into your character, then (1) you will be found trustworthy, and (2) you will make everyone better.

Trustworthy: Being trusted will also make you more credible and respected. The opposite, being untrustworthy, is an absolute curse. Being untrustworthy may ruin a relationship or prevent you from getting into a community, club, or group. Being untrustworthy may cause you to get fired from your job or kicked off the team. And once you are found to be untrustworthy, it is difficult, and sometimes impossible, to get reinstated or to earn back someone's trust.

Making Everyone Better: Believe it or not, lies are temporary fixes that ruin relationships and organizations. But when you speak the Truth, your relationships and organizations get stronger. Consider the bonds you have with your closest friends, because they know you well. They know your faults and flaws, and yet they still love you. They tell you the Truth, even when you don't want to hear it. But because they tell you the Truth, your relationship continues to get stronger and stronger. Consider a sports team. If the team can be honest about their performance, they can learn how to get better or faster. But if they lie to each other and say that they are doing well when they are not, they will lose, over and over.

Special Forces Training

Imagine you just finished Special Operations Selection and Assessment. The training cadre pulls you to the side of the formation. He looks you straight in the eye and tells you a lie. He tells you what you want to hear: "I don't know why you didn't get selected. I thought you did a great job. Nonetheless, I put in a good word for you, but it didn't work out. Sorry about that, brother. I hope to see you back for selection next year." God forbid this would ever happen.

The more likely scenario is that the training cadre pulls you to the side of the formation. He looks you straight in the eye and tells you what you don't want to hear. "Check this out, candidate. You are not getting selected. And I threw the final vote not to select you. You don't have to blame anyone else; you can blame me. I see that you have a lot of heart, and we can all see that you 'put out' and gave 100%. But you just didn't measure up to the guys on your left and right. So, I'm sending you back to the force to get a bit stronger and faster. Take the next year to develop as a soldier and to get more physically fit. And I'll see you back here in twelve months."

It is obvious that telling the soldier the Truth is going to hurt him. No one like to hear that they have enough heart to be in the Special Operations community but they still lack the strength. But by telling the Truth, the soldier knows what he needs to focus on and will come back next year stronger and more prepared.

Dishonest Product Labels

It isn't hard to find examples of dishonest businesses. It hurts me how dishonorable so many industries are these days. We are now forced to read the small print in all our contracts and warranties. Regardless of the name of the company or what the front of the package says, you have to read the ingredients list on all food products these days just to make sure that you are, in fact, eating just food. "Designed in America" means that it was made by slave labor in China. "Get Ripped in Ten Days" is guaranteed *not* to eliminate years of poor diet and unhealthy lifestyle choices.

The Alcoholic Brother

Imagine a brother who has an alcohol problem. He has gained a lot of weight and his relationships and work performance are suffering. You can ignore his alcohol issues and or sweep it under the table. But the Truth is, his addiction is unhealthy and unsafe. A weak person pretends that his brother doesn't have a drinking problem. He talks about it and about him behind his back. He doesn't want to hurt his feelings. But the strong person confronts his brother. He tells him he is destroying his future and that he has gotten fat. He offers help. He is there for him. Which type of person tells the Truth? Which person has the type of character you would want on a Special Operations team?

Individual Training Plan: (PTREXAR)

It isn't hard to plan to always speak the Truth. You simply need to make a decision and Commitment to yourself that you are going to be honest. It is more likely that you have one or two areas in your life where you are lying to yourself. And so, I recommend that you find these areas where you need to be truthful. Identify where and when you are not being truthful and make a plan to be truthful. Are you lying to yourself about how awesome you are? Confront reality, make a plan to improve, and get after it. Are you lying about how strong you are? Make a plan to get there. Are you lying to yourself that you are making good decisions? Figure it out, and start making good decisions.

Now is the point where you need to take a break from this book, sit down with a piece of paper, and make a plan on how you are going to train / develop the mindset of Truthfulness. Use the below questions to help you make your plan.

If you are going to skip this section, then please at least answer the first question: Where am I the least Truthful?

Plan:
- Where am I the least Truthful?
- How can I improve my Truthfulness in that area?
- List three things I can do to increase my Truthfulness.
    - #1:
    - #2:
    - #3:
- How do I plan to accomplish each of the above?
    - Training Tasks / Behaviors / Actions?
    - Frequency of Training?
    - Milestones / Phases?
- How or where or in what situations can I rehearse showing or displaying Truth?
- What is the purpose of being Truthful?
- What is my ultimate Goal / End-State regarding Truth?
- How can I evaluate if my Truth training is working?

Train: Go out there and get to work. Start today. Do what you planned (above) to do. Train like you fight. Don't make this easy on yourself. Make your training harder and more difficult, so that when it becomes time to execute your goal, you will be overly prepared.

Rehearse: Put yourself in situations where you will be able to demonstrate Truthfulness.

Execute: Execute that final display of Truth for which you have been planning. Accomplish your goal.

Analyze: Assess if your Truthfulness has grown and developed. Analyze how effective your training plan was. What did you do wrong during this PTREXAR cycle? How can you improve next time?

Repeat: Now get out there and do the whole PTREXAR cycle again! Get even better!

3: Competence

I met Adam, a Major in Marine Special Operations, late in 2008 at the Combined Joint Special Operations Command – Afghanistan (CJSOTF-A). I was the J35 Future Operations Officer, and Adam was on loan to our office for a couple of months to learn about the rigorous planning and tedious approval process for SOF missions in Afghanistan. Adam was going to be the commander of a MARSOC (Marine Special Operations Company) deploying to Western Afghanistan in June of 2009. I was very impressed with Adam's Competence and professionalism during our time in Bagram and wished him nothing but success and "good hunting" during his upcoming deployment.

After ten months in Afghanistan, I redeployed in January 2009, took two weeks of leave to go snowboarding at Lake Tahoe, and then reported back in to the 7th Special Forces Group (Airborne) to see if they decided what my next job would be. My boss informed me that I would be the Executive Officer of 3rd Battalion, and that we were scheduled to go establish a Special Operations Task Force and presence in Western Afghanistan in June. We were going to command and control one Special Forces company and two MARSOCs. A week later I was reunited with

Adam, who was in command of one of the MARSOCs, as we assembled all of the leaders to begin some mission analysis and planning. A few weeks later, we were back in Afghanistan for a site survey, and by May I was living in a tent at a small firebase outside of Herat, a contentious and unconquerable wasteland since the times of Alexander the Great.

Adam had been assigned to "work" the area in the vicinity of Farah. And absolutely did he work it. What transpired over the course of the next sixty days was what I would call textbook-perfect counter-insurgency. Adams knew from his time with me at the CJSOTF-A that his paperwork had to be in order. This is a sad Truth, but the Truth nonetheless. And it was in order. His Concepts of the Operation (CONOPs) were perfect, and he properly request in advanced every asset and enabler available in theater.

Farah had long been under Taliban control, and the people of Farah were tired of living under their suppressive regime. After setting the stage for two months with humanitarian outreach missions, presence patrols, intelligence gathering, and free medical clinics, Adam assembled his entire MARSOC for a comprehensive Taliban clearance mission, which targeted dozens of Taliban strongholds. Day and night for two weeks, the city was a war zone. Adam was enabled by every asset in the task force: Close Air Support (CAS), artillery, radio jamming and messaging, civil affairs, medical teams. Even the Chaplain got in on the action. It was a dangerous symphony that Adam flawlessly orchestrated, using every instrument at his service. As soon as a neighborhood was cleared of the Taliban, Adam brought in Afghan police to maintain order, and distributed medical care to the poor and food for the hungry. By the end of the two weeks, the city was back under the control and leadership of the Government of the Islamic Republic of Afghanistan (GIRoA). There was celebration in the streets. Adam spent the rest of his deployment building schools (for girls, too), developing and rebuilding infrastructure, and advising the GIRoA leaders as life went back to normal.

I have to say that in all my three deployments in Afghanistan, Adam did it the best. He orchestrated the textbook-perfect counter-insurgency operation, kicked out the Taliban, and restored basic life freedoms and privileges to thousands of the people of Farah. To this day, when I think of Adam, I think of Competence. Well done, brother.

Definition & Considerations

Simply put, Competence is "the <u>ability to do something well</u>."[2]

It is further defined as "the quality or state of having <u>sufficient knowledge, judgment, skill, or strength</u>."[3]

We see from these two definitions is that <u>Competence is about knowledge and ability</u>. Rarely, a job requires only knowledge. In that case, an employee can be competent simply by knowing and understanding all aspects of their job. But most occupations also have physical and skill requirements. These must be mastered before someone can be declared competent.

<u>Competence requires diligence</u>. No one wakes up one day and they are completely competent. **They learn it and earn it**.

I'm putting Competence at the beginning of our list of Special Operations Mindsets because <u>Competence is essential</u>. What makes Special Operators so exceptional is that they are great at

---

[2] https://www.oxfordlearnersdictionaries.com/definition/english/competence
[3] https://www.merriam-webster.com/dictionary/competence

what they do. They are knowledgeable, capable, and competent. You could never be a Special Operator without the aptitude to problem-solve, understand and use tactics, shoot your weapon perfectly, move in a safe way, and communicate with other members of your team and with headquarters. The skills and abilities which members of the elite Special Operations community rely upon are the result of endless evolutions of deliberate Planning, Training, Rehearsing, Executing, Analyzing, and Repeating. PTREXAR is how they build and maintain their individual and collective Competence.

What it is

Regardless of your field of work, in order to be competent you need to master the basics of that field. It is not just enough to know the basics; you must master them. And this goes for knowledge and abilities. Let's start with knowledge.

Knowledge is required for Competence. The ignorant employee is a liability. The competent leader is an asset. Knowledge of the basics is what I like to call knowing what is "inside the box." These are facts, laws, rules, policies, doctrines. Most people understand and are comfortable with what is inside the box. But in order to think or work "outside the box," you need to know and master "what is inside the box."

On top of knowing information, most occupations also require <u>mastery of basic skills</u>. Skills come from doing. This means that Competence is a result of experience and training. Chapter One discusses the PTREXAR model for training. If you want to be competent, then you must deliberately train and drill yourself into mastery.

What it isn't

Competence isn't "faking it" to impress your boss. Competence isn't lying to yourself about your skills or knowledge. We just finished a chapter about Truth. If you are truly competent, no one can take it away from you or claim that you are not.

Competence isn't about show and perceptions. It isn't about number of followers and subscribers. It is about knowledge and abilities.

Best Indicators Of

<u>The best indicator of Competence is peace</u>. This may strike you as amusing, but I assure you that it is true. Regardless of your field of work, imagine that you have to brief your bosses. If you are incompetent, then you worry about what they

will ask and if they will find a weakness in your plan or logic or project. But if you are competent, then you have peace. There is no one who knows about this plan or project or mission more than you. No one can "stump the chump." No one can make you look bad because you own the knowledge and have mastered the skills. And even if they do have some strong questions and or some new ideas, you welcome any opportunity to go from good to great.

Another indicator of Competence is <u>the ability to analyze a reference</u>. An amateur does something and doesn't know why. A professional is able to do something and quote the reference (facts, laws, rules, policies, doctrines …) which prescribes that type of activity. But only a competent master is able to quote a reference and analyze ways to use or not use it, ways to ignore aspects of them or how to make it better.

When I was in Harvard, my professors assigned hundreds of pages of reading each week. These were the references, and it was assumed that after reading them, we knew them. We never discussed what these references said. We only analyzed the references as compared to other references, or looking back through history, or how they apply to the contemporary operational environment. The following year I went to the Command and General Staff College. Each week we were assigned homework. These, too, were references. And then when we came to class, we regurgitated what the references said for eight hours a day. We were taught to regurgitate, not analyze. It was such a terrible and painful year. I was intellectually bored to death. My instructors only asked us to regurgitate. They never asked us to analyze. What a shame. All of the other Majors in the course with me were masters of the basics… they were professionals, who could only regurgitate references. None of them were competent masters, able to analyze references. And this was sad.

A final indicator of Competence is the <u>ability to multitask</u>. You are able to do one complex skill while simultaneously thinking about, planning for, or working on a second skill. Once you have mastered shooting your rifle, you then start shooting your rifle while you walk, then run. Then you do it at night with visible lasers. Then you do it at night with infrared lasers and night-vision goggles. Then you do it from a moving vehicle.

Too Much or Too Little

<u>Too little Competence, and you are not legit</u>. Going back to the chapter on Truth … no one can ever master everything. So, if you are not an expert, then rely upon and use the expertise of those

around you. Never fake Competence when you don't have it. If you are caught, it will destroy your credibility. Simply be honest with yourself and your team and use PTREXAR to develop your skills and knowledge to the point of Competence.

It is almost impossible to have too much Competence. Knowing and mastering is always a great thing. Imagine how much more successful and effective your business or team would be if everyone had mastered the required knowledge and skills of your enterprise. But I will say that having too much Competence can sometimes be counterproductive to progress. This is usually the result of people with "know it all" syndrome. They are such experts with regard to knowledge and skills that they overthink and overanalyze every piece of minutia. It is not their Competence that makes them a hindrance. They are hindrances because the way they process and overthink a situation leads them along time-wasting tangents. If members of your team have "know it all" syndrome, then I recommend that you try to get them involved [distracted] in only one specific aspect of the project, while others can focus on mission accomplishment.

Implications Of

If you are competent in your field of work, then you are going to be (1) trusted, (2) respected, and (3) your team will perform better.

<u>Trusted</u>: A faker or liar is never trusted. But a competent man or woman is valued and trusted.

<u>Respected</u>: Competence is respected. Everyone knows this. It is so frustrating to waste time with people who do not know their job. It is so delightful to have a discussion with or a recommendation from an expert. When you are competent in knowledge and skill, your colleagues and superiors will take notice. This will enhance your credibility and your reputation.

<u>Better Team Performance</u>: If your Competence sets the standard within your organization, others will rise to join you. This will build an organization of excellence, significantly increasing your performance along the way.

How It's Built

<u>Competence is built by learning and doing</u>. You can learn from other's successes. You can learn from other's mistakes. You can learn from reading. You can learn from doing. All of this is active. You will not magically be able to quote

regulations and specifications if you don't study them. Your skills will never improve if you don't apply a deliberate training program. Competence is active. And because it is possible to forget or to lose your skills, Competence is continuous. You must continuously learn and study to improve your knowledge-based Competence. And you must continually train and drill to improve your skills.

Shoot – Move – Communicate

A soldier is always required to know how to "shoot, move, and communicate." He is able to do this, and some even do this well. But a Special Operator **has mastered** these skills. He **has mastered** shooting his weapon, day and night, with scopes and with night-vision devices, until it all becomes second nature, and he almost never misses. He **has mastered** moving as an individual, team, in a vehicle, jumping out of an airplane, or navigating in the dark as a part of a subsurface scuba team. He has state-of-the-art communication devices and **has mastered** how to use all of them, in daylight and in the dark. He **has mastered** basic skills and abilities.

The Competent Car Salesman

An average car salesman doesn't know very much. He will know the price. He might remember some of the car's history. He can show you how "cool" a car looks and tell you that it is fast. But a competent car salesman has mastered the basics. He **knows** the history of the car and all its capabilities and technologies. He **knows** the rules for guarantees. He **knows** how to fill out the paperwork. And he **knows** how to honorably engage and talk to potential customers.

Passive or Competent Fathers

We all know chaotic families led by a passive and incompetent father. The mother is forced to step up into his leadership void. These families are fun to hang out with … but being a part of them is painful. They are messy, undisciplined, always late, in debt, and they always seem to be chasing the latest shiny object. On the other hand, the competent father has mastered family leadership. He has a man plan. He knows how to budget, forecast, and take care of the physical and emotional needs of his family. Living under the roof of a competent father is a privilege few have these days.

Individual Training / Development Plan: (PTREXAR)

Now is the point where you need to take a break from this book, sit down with a piece of paper, and make a plan on how you are going to train / develop the mindset of Competence. Use the below questions to help you make your plan.

If you are going to skip this section, then please at least answer the first question: Where am I the least competent?

<u>Plan</u>:
- Where am I the least competent?
- How can I improve my Competence in that area?
- List three things I can do to increase my Competence:
    - #1:
    - #2:
    - #3:
- How do I plan to accomplish each of the above?
    - Training Tasks / Behaviors / Actions?
    - Frequency of Training?
    - Milestones / Phases?

- How or where or in what situations can I rehearse showing or displaying Competence?
- What is the purpose of being competent?
- What is my ultimate Goal / End-State regarding Competence?
- How can I evaluate if my Competence training is working?

Train: Go out there and get to work. Start today. Do what you planned (above) to do. Train like you fight. Don't make this easy on yourself. Make your training harder and more difficult, so that when it becomes time to execute your goal, you will be overly prepared.

Rehearse: Put yourself in situations where you will be able to demonstrate Competence.

Execute: Execute that final display of Competence for which you have been planning. Accomplish your goal.

Analyze: Assess if your Competence has grown and developed. Analyze how effective your training plan was. What did you do wrong during this PTREXAR cycle? How can you improve next time?

<u>Repeat</u>: Now get out there and do the whole PTREXAR cycle again! Get even better!

4: Confidence

Many people would argue that Confidence is the most important mindset of SOF. But I don't think so. I would much rather be around someone with little Confidence, but who was competent and always right, than to be around someone with a lot of Confidence who is neither competent nor correct. Yet, I must point out, that when you are competent and always right, it almost always creates Confidence. And that is why there aren't Special Operators with self-esteem issues. When you constantly and consistently build your Competence through accomplishments and finish hard training, the automatic byproduct is self-esteem and Confidence.

I want to tell you the story about the most confident man I ever met. Let's call him Brent. I met Brent when we were both Majors at the NATO International Security Assistance Force (ISAF) headquarters in Kabul, Afghanistan during the beginning of my second tour to Afghanistan. I was assigned to serve a few months in Kabul as the liaison between the Combined Joint Special Operations Task Force – Afghanistan (CJSOTF-A) and ISAF. Brent had served there for six months and as his replacement, we had seven days of overlap for him to teach me everything he knew, before he returned to Fort Bragg.

Brent had served as a Special Forces Team Leader in the very first days of the war after the 9/11 attacks on the World Trade Center and the Pentagon. He had already proven his bravery and tactical Courage, but working at ISAF headquarters was something new. As the liaison officer, Brent had to represent the CJSOTF-A at major planning events and to brief the ISAF Commander or Deputy Commander for permission to execute certain missions.

When he was in planning events, he was always the lowest-ranking person in the room. During my week of our overlap, I watched him tell a roomful of Generals and Colonels "no" a dozen times. Here are two examples.

"Sir, that mission is worthless. The second you go into a small village with fifty tanks, the Taliban are going to take off their black turbans, hide their weapons, and then come outside and thank you for liberating them. A week later they are going to be back to business ambushing small logistic patrols. There will be no long-term effect for that mission. I recommend against wasting everyone's time."

And of course, they did the mission anyways. With no long-term effect.

"Sir, that is a terrible idea. We can't pull ten Special Ops teams from ten important and dispersed missions where we are building partner capacity in the hope of one day working ourselves out of a job to make a clearing force in an empty and unimportant valley. Use a company of infantry or an unmanned aerial vehicle (UAV) to see if there is anyone living there."

They sent 120 infantrymen who walked along a huge valley for a week with nothing to report. It was classic mismanagement at the highest levels, and Brent would never let their incompetence interrupt CJSOTF-A productivity.

Not only was Brent confident when planning, he was also totally confident and relaxed whenever he briefed the ISAF Commander or Deputy Commander for permission to do a mission. He always got a kick out of waking up the Generals.

"Hey Chris, check this out. Last-minute intel is leading us to do this mission. Let's wake up the General and go get his permission."

But the most important part of Brent's Confidence came from his brazen Courage. He had to show me around to the other headquarters and key sites in Kabul. We went to this compound for a planning meeting and then to that compound to request a special enabler. Then we rehearsed different routes to the airport, then to another compound to share some intel. After reaching one remote compound, I asked Brent: "I'm sorry. I can't remember what we are doing here. Is this another intel meeting?"

"No, Chris. They serve Mexican food every Tuesday for lunch out here. I like to stop by for tacos."

I was aghast. We assumed so much personal risk driving through Kabul in our armored Land Rover, just to get Mexican food. I remember making a mental note about how high Brent's threshold for risk was.

Despite being the lowest-ranking man in the planning room, Brent had the Confidence to plan what would work and to try to stop or shut down anything that wouldn't. Brent had the Confidence to wake the General up at two in the morning to get permission to execute a time-sensitive mission. Brent had the Confidence to navigate the streets of Kabul, and the Courage to do it alone and unafraid.

Brent's Confidence was rooted in absolute Competence. And that is how he got away with it. It was real.

As you can imagine, I had some big shoes to fill. And although I am a bit humbler, by nature, than Brent, I will brag that several months later I was replaced not by one man, but by a team of three. And they were all shocked that we drove through Kabul alone and unafraid just for Taco Tuesday.

Definition & Considerations

Confidence is defined as "a belief in your own ability to <u>do</u> things and <u>be</u> successful."[4]

Without being too philosophical, I want to break up this definition into two parts: (1) doing and (2) being. For the sake of simplicity, let's say that Confidence in doing things is very much related to Competence and Training, while Confidence for being is very much related to self-esteem.

I want to highlight that this is a belief. It isn't factual. It has nothing to do with reality or Truth. This is why so many beautiful women think they are ugly and why so many idiot men think they are awesome. They have a false belief, which reflects in their Confidence. If you believe in yourself but are incompetent or an idiot, you still have Confidence. But if you are Competent and

---

[4] https://www.oxfordlearnersdictionaries.com/definition/english/Confidence

capable, but don't believe in yourself, you don't have Confidence.

What it is

Confidence is a belief in yourself. It is your self-assessment. It is always best if your Confidence is built upon an honest (Chapter 2: Truth) valuation of your capabilities and abilities (Chapter 3: Competence & Chapter 1: Training).

<u>Confidence can be focalized</u> and associated with skill. Just like Competence, it is impossible to be confident in all things. For example, you may be a great swimmer, but you are a terrible chess player. In this case, you would logically have Confidence in your swimming skills but lack Confidence in your chess skills.

<u>Confidence can also be generalized</u> towards your being. This means that you are confident in yourself, as a human, regardless of a certain skill or ability. This is the type of holistic Confidence that is based upon valuation. You value one skill or one voice or one characteristic over another. Let me explain.

Imagine that your father, who you love and respect, is a professional chess player who has told you all throughout your childhood that being a great chess player is the most important skill in the world. Regardless of being a great swimmer (from the example above), you are going to have Confidence issues because you are not a great chess player. You value his voice, and his voice says that being a good chess player is the premier characteristic of being and self-worth.

If you value your parent's opinion, your self-esteem will be a result of their approval or values, regardless of your skills and abilities. If you value the Bible, your Confidence comes from being a loved child of God, regardless of your skills or abilities. If you value money, your self-esteem is significantly influence by your wealth or lack thereof.

I think that the healthiest Confidence is a result of both doing (skills and abilities) and being (values).

The Hundred-Dollar Bill

While we are on the subject of value, I want to quickly give you the illustration of the hundred-dollar bill. The U.S. bank note with the picture of Benjamin Franklin is worth 100 U.S. Dollars. Always. It doesn't matter if the bank note is old or new, it is always worth 100 U.S. Dollars.

Several years ago, a friend of the family was having a low point in her life. Her work colleagues were being especially mean to her, and her self-esteem was at an all-time low. I pulled out a hundred-dollar bill and showed it to her. I asked her how much it was worth.

She replied, "One hundred dollars."

Next, I crumbled it in my hands. After flattening it back out, I showed it again to her, asking what it was worth.

Again, she replied, "One hundred dollars."

Then I crumpled up the hundred-dollar bill and threw it on the ground, stepping on it several times. It was a bit overdramatic, but she got the point. I picked up the crumpled and stepped-on hundred-dollar bill and held it up to her, asking a final time what it was worth.

With tears in her eyes, she replied, "One hundred dollars."

She obviously learned the point of my illustration. As I flattened out the hundred-dollar bill, I explained further: "Regardless of being flat and new, or being crumpled and stepped on, this one-hundred-dollar bill is worth one hundred dollars. It will never be worth less. So even if your dumb work colleagues are treating you poorly and stepping on you … you are still valuable and maintain your worth ... which is priceless in God's eyes. So, stop listening to your stupid colleagues and start focusing on your real value."

What it isn't

<u>Confidence is not arrogance</u>. In fact, the best and most capable people I have met have all been quite humble.

<u>Confidence should not be false or fake</u>. I use the word "should" instead of "is" because I have met some truly confident people who are not capable at all. Their Confidence is based upon falseness. But because they value this falseness, they have a lot of self-esteem. Let me give you an example. Imagine that you were a spoiled rich kid. Your parents paid people to take care of you and to keep you out of trouble. You always got what you wanted. You were never disciplined, or rebuked, or told that you failed. You grew up thinking that you were the best at everything. As an adult, you have several failed businesses. But in spite of your failures and incompetence, some of your businesses succeed. And so, you believe that you are better and smarter and more successful than anyone else, and your self-esteem reflects your inflated self-opinion. You are the emperor who isn't wearing clothes.

Another common example of false or fake self-esteem is seen in the younger generations. Imagine that your parents don't care about the Truth (Chapter 2: Truth) and tell you that you are the best at everything. You never develop skills and abilities (Chapter 3: Competence) because you get a trophy for last place and your parents tell you that you are the best swimmer and chess player in the city. Then you surround yourself with social media friends and fans who only tell you what you want to hear and who agree with you about everything. No wonder you have high self-esteem and high Confidence.

And just so you don't think that I am picking on the younger generations, it is great when someone has Confidence. Better to be too confident than lack Confidence. But yet, Confidence based upon a true analysis of skills, abilities, and being is much more honorable.

I have also observed that many leaders who lack essential abilities, usually Competence and intelligence, become tyrants to overcompensate for their lack of aptitudes. Most of these men had a lot of self-esteem and Confidence. I can only assert that their Confidence was also faked, reinforced by the lies they tell themselves and believe.

Self-Doubt: I want to add in a quick discussion about overcoming self-doubt. We all have times of self-doubt. Sometimes it is legit and sometimes it isn't.

When self-doubt antagonizes a person who is actually capable, it must be dominated and beat down by Truth; the Truth that you are capable; the Truth that you have been trained, educated and prepared for this very day; the Truth that like a 100-dollar bill, you are independently and inherently valuable. If you are doubting yourself before a briefing, then remind yourself that you have rehearsed the presentation five times and that no one on earth knows this information better than you. Be nervous. But don't doubt yourself. If you doubt yourself and your ability to lead a team, then remind yourself that no one knows more about the mission or project than you. If you are doubting yourself after getting into a confrontation or an argument, then ground yourself in the Truth. If what you said was the Truth, spoken with honor for the right reasons, then stop doubting.

Legitimate self-doubt haunts the person who realizes that he is in over his head. A wise person who is honest with himself about his abilities doesn't call this self-doubt. He simply calls it the Truth. The fact is, you can't be an expert at everything. Confident people are okay with this. But for the person who has been lying to himself about his abilities and who grounds his false Confidence in deception, self-doubt is at least a step in the right direction towards Truth and rehabilitation. Maybe one day they will stop lying to themselves and others. If you aren't confident about something, then admit it; ask for help, ask for an explanation. This isn't weakness. Never pretend that you get it when you don't. Never tap dance when you don't know the answer. Honorable and secure people tell the Truth. They don't fake it.

Best Indicators Of

The <u>best indicator of Confidence is ability</u>. If you have trained (PTREXAR) and developed your abilities (Competence), then you will develop genuine Confidence. There is no substitute for abilities. And there is no substitute for continuous training and development.

Another important indicator of true Confidence is your <u>ability to accept criticism</u>. A genuinely confident person knows what he or she is capable of. They know their value. And yet, they also know that they are not perfect and can always learn or improve in certain skills, abilities, or characteristics. A person who has false Confidence will panic in the face of legitimate criticism. A person with real Confidence will appreciate criticism as it will make them better.

A final indicator of Confidence is what I like to call the "<u>Critical Play Factor</u>." When there is time enough for one last play in the game, do you defer to others to make the critical play or do you make it yourself? When you need to do something critical to the war or battle or business or game, do you jump in and take control? Or do you stand by on the sidelines and watch the real players perform? <u>A man of Confidence wants the figurative ball in his court every time. He never wants to defer Responsibility for the victory</u>.

Too Much or Too Little

If you have too much Confidence, you are not based in reality. Your perception of your abilities doesn't match what you can actually do or back up. I see this a lot in the younger generations. They think they are wonderful and amazing and are always shocked when they don't get hired, don't get admitted, don't get promoted. Rather than being objective about their skills and abilities, they only focus on the subjective praise and reinforcement from their circle of codependents and enablers. My recommendation to the next generation of leaders is to focus on Chapter 2: Truth. Learn to be objective about your abilities and competencies ... and build Confidence based upon experiences and Truth, rather than upon what your social media followers tell you.

A trend I am noticing in Western cultures is that so many people are becoming overweight and obese. It doesn't look good. It doesn't feel good. And for sure, it isn't healthy. Nonetheless, you can't go anywhere these days without seeing overweight women confidently going about their day in overly stressed black yoga pants. It is as if the slimming effect of black leggings makes women forget that they have twenty to one hundred extra pounds of body fat that doesn't belong. They don't have anyone who lovingly speaks the Truth to them. They base their Confidence not upon what they see in the mirror or what their scale tells them, but upon the subjective praise and reinforcement from their circle of codependents and enablers. Honestly, I would much rather see a woman with too much Confidence than without Confidence. But it is getting out of control that unhealthy and undisciplined (see the next chapter) people are walking around with their heads up high.

Too much Confidence also creates arrogance. This is why it is always important to have a humble assessment of yourself. No matter how awesome you are, there will always be someone better, stronger, faster, smarter. Even if it takes a few years, you will always be replaced. So be confident in your abilities and worth, but don't let your Confidence lead you down the path to arrogance.

On the other hand, if you have too little Confidence, then you will never stick up for yourself or achieve what you have the potential to achieve. If you don't believe in yourself, then you will never push yourself to take a leap of faith, to start a new business, to ask for the promotion, or to insist on being treated better.

Implications Of

If you are confident in yourself and your abilities, then you are going to (1) perform better, (2) be more successful, and (3) be less afraid of failure, and (4) be more prepared for future challenges.

<u>Perform Better</u>: Because a legitimate Confidence is based upon real ability, a person with genuine skills will always perform better than someone with fewer skills or who is not as well trained.

<u>Be More Successful</u>: Performing better than those around you will lead to your success. Once you are recognized as a winner, you will be chosen to perform during future missions, games, or business opportunities and promotions. Success leads to more success.

Be Less Afraid of Failure: A confident man is not afraid to fail. He knows his worth and abilities and is able to recover and bounce back from a failure. He learns from his mistakes and uses what he has learned to be more prepared for future endeavors. Failure doesn't make a loser. Fear of failure makes a loser. Not learning from your mistakes makes you a loser.

Be More Prepared for Future Challenges: If you are a confident and capable person, you are prepared for any future challenge. A future challenge might not be in your field of expertise. But because you are a proven and capable leader, able to accept criticism and admit that you need help from other experts on your team, you will figure out how to succeed.

How It's Built

You build Confidence by doing hard things. You set goals and you work hard to accomplish them. I think this is the easiest way to describe the process of building Confidence. Sometimes, however, you will set a goal and not reach it. But in striving towards the goal, you build Confidence in your abilities.

You can also build Confidence by being loved and valued. This is the illustration of the hundred-dollar bill. Children who know they are loved and valued are much more confident than those who are neglected. Members of a team who are honored and valued have more Confidence than those who are marginalized. This is one reason why members of gangs are so dangerous. They finally get acceptance and recognition through the gang, and in turn they are ignorantly loyal.

Members of Special Operations do hard things. They set almost impossible fitness and performance goals and do everything within their power to accomplish these goals. They are honored and respected and valued as a member of the team. We have heard countless times that a soldier fights "for my brother on my left and right." When you are so trusted and valued as a member of the team that your teammates would fight and die for you, then you know you are loved and valued. And this produces a Confidence which is hard to replicate in the civilian world.

It is absurd to have more self-worth because you can run a marathon. What does running for a few hours have with being a good father or mother, student or business leader? Nothing? Everything? It isn't the fact that you can run for four hours without stopping that makes you a confident person. It is the fact that you set a hard goal, trained for it, and accomplished it which helps you build Confidence. And doing this over and over in various ways teaches you that with enough training and preparation, you can do and accomplish anything.

Team Confidence

After years of schools and deployments, I was very confident in my skills and abilities. Yet I always knew that my success was the result of the amazing teams of which I was always a part. And this kept and keeps me humble. Knowing that you have survived and sometimes even flourished during some of the most difficult training and circumstances in the world is strengthening. But <u>it is even more empowering when you know that teams and companies of equally trained men have your back</u>. Confidence, based upon abilities and value, is empowering. And a team of confident people is almost invincible. This is why we study and try to learn from the Special Operations mindset.

The Overly Confident Boss

For our business application, let's take a look at a bad example. A boss is overconfident. The success of his company is the result of his employees, in spite of his leadership. He decides to acquire a failing business, one which he believes has potential to be profitable. His advisors tell him that this is not a good idea and warn him not to overextend himself and the company. He has Confidence that he can make it happen. But he didn't do any research to realize that the market is oversaturated with similar but successful businesses like the one he is acquiring. He is confident that based upon his current success, he can make his new acquisition successful. He is wrong. Despite his honorable employees giving their 100% effort to support the new undertaking, the new business acquisition fails. And in doing so, it borrows and consumes all the assets of the first business. The man files for bankruptcy yet remains confident for the rest of his life. And of course, he would remain confident ... his Confidence is not based in ability or Truth or reality. He views his failed business as a result of his employees sabotaging his efforts. He is the victim.

The Industrious Student

A young man studied hard and was able to graduate six months early. After finishing his education, he got a job at a prestigious international firm in his city where he works hard and continues to learn his new craft. As soon as he got his job, he moved out of his parents' house to "become his own man." The money was tight but he was disciplined and lived in accordance with his budget. Now, in his late twenties, he owns an apartment and is beginning to serve as a competent and trusted member of the prototype development team. His integrity and Competence have earned him the Trust and respect of his colleagues and superiors. He has worked and trained hard to be competent. He has set hard goals with his studies, his work, and his budget. And he has accomplished all of them. Although humble, this young man is confident ... and ready for the next challenges and phases and successes of life.

Individual Training / Development Plan: (PTREXAR)

Now is the point where you need to take a break from this book, sit down with a piece of paper, and make a plan on how you are going to train / develop the mindset of Confidence. Use the below questions to help you make your plan.

If you are going to skip this section, then please at least answer the first question: Where am I the least confident?

<u>Plan</u>:
- Where am I the least confident?
- How can I improve my Confidence in that area?
- List three things I can do to increase my Confidence:
    - # 1:

- o #2:
- o #3:
- How do I plan to accomplish each of the above?
    - o Training Tasks / Behaviors / Actions?
    - o Frequency of Training?
    - o Milestones / Phases?
- How or where or in what situations can I rehearse showing or displaying Confidence?
- What is the purpose of developing Confidence?
- What is my ultimate Goal / End-State regarding Confidence?
- How can I evaluate if my Confidence training is working?

Train: Go out there and get to work. Start today. Do what you planned (above) to do. Train like you fight. Don't make this easy on yourself. Make your training harder and more difficult, so that when it becomes time to execute your goal, you will be overly prepared.

Rehearse: Put yourself in situations where you will be able to demonstrate Confidence.

<u>Execute</u>: Execute that final display of Confidence for which you have been planning. Accomplish your goal.

<u>Analyze</u>: Assess if your Confidence has grown and developed. Analyze how effective your training plan was. What did you do wrong during this PTREXAR cycle? How can you improve next time?

<u>Repeat</u>: Now get out there and do the whole PTREXAR cycle again! Get even better!

5: Discipline

As a young Lieutenant in 101st Airborne Division (Air Assault), I was able to rent an inexpensive apartment with another Lieutenant in my BDE. Our normal Monday through Friday routine was pretty pathetic. We would get up at 0530, drive to Ft. Campbell for morning Physical Training (PT) and then stay and work all day. One of us would pick up some Mexican food or Taco Bell and bring it home after work. We would then watch his TV, usually ESPN, until we couldn't stay awake. Then we would go to sleep and wake up the next morning at 0530 to do it all again.

When he got married to his high school sweetheart, I moved out and got my own apartment. I had so much free time after work that the month I moved out I started mountain biking again, started Taekwondo, bought a motorcycle (dirt bike), joined the skydiving club at Fort Campbell, and read four books. It was amazing how much better my life was when I stopped watching TV after work. If only I would have been more disciplined during the first year that I lived at Fort Campbell.

I continued to live without a TV for fifteen more years. Doing so freed up so much more time to do, learn, and accomplish. My wife eventually put her foot down… and so, at thirty-seven years old, I bought our first TV. In fact, this year I bought our second TV, a Smart TV. It is amazing. We have an impressive, entertaining, and educational variety of viewing opportunities. But the Truth is, I could care less. I'm not saying that TV is bad. But I will say that unless you have the Discipline to limit your TV intake, you will waste your life in front of that amazing piece of technology.

Definition & Considerations

Webster's dictionary defines Discipline as "<u>self-control</u>" and "<u>control gained by enforcing obedience or order</u>."[5] Most of what we will focus on is the self-control implications of Discipline. However, we will also discuss the control (of behavior, of team activities) gained by enforcing obedience and order.

What it is

<u>Discipline is doing what you know is right</u>. A simple example is exercising. We know that exercising a few hours a week is great for your health. But we are all lazy by nature and it is so simple to stay on the couch and enjoy the million shows and series and movies and videos available via your Smart TV or electronic devices.

---

[5] https://www.merriam-webster.com/dictionary/discipline

<u>Discipline is also not doing what you know is wrong</u>. An easy-to-understand example of this is eating junk food. We all know that junk food is bad for you. But it tastes so good. And a cheeseburger with fries and a large Coke is okay for me every once and a while. Right?

Discipline is using logic or passion to gain control of a situation or yourself in a way contrary to your natural inclinations. A great example of this is when someone is rude to you. Your natural instinct may be to be rude back. Or to fight. But if you are disciplined, you will not let your anger overtake and escalate the situation. You deescalate the situation and handle it in a more civilized and professional manner.

What it isn't

<u>Discipline is not being a robot</u>. It always makes me laugh when I see an overly enthusiastic young soldier or Marine straight out of basic training. They walk and stand in awkward and funny positions. Their posture is amazing. They absolutely accept and celebrate their new role as a Marine. They think that standing at parade rest when around civilians and their family members at graduation demonstrates their newly earned Discipline. Hollywood also likes to show Marines as robots. "Sir, yes sir." "Roger that." This

isn't proving that you are disciplined. It is proving that you are not smart enough to know that you should behave one way when in front of your drill sergeants, and that you should act another when around normal humans.

<u>Discipline is not being a slave to process</u>. Processes and standing / standard operating procedures (SOPs) are guidelines which help you accomplish the mission and ensure people know how work gets done. But sometimes these SOPs become biblical law, when they should only have been guidelines. A great example of this is the conventional military mentality. When I was in the 101st Airborne Division, we had to eat and sleep in our helmets. We were not allowed to wear our Gortex rain jackets because only the "support guys" wear Gortex. When we were in garrison, we had to do push-ups and sit-ups and run four miles every single day. We weren't super disciplined; we were stupid disciplined.

Discipline is <u>not waking up at 0430 every morning</u> and preaching to the entire world that they also need to wake up at 0430. Science and countless studies have shown that Circadian Rhythm and "Sleep Pressure" (Adenosine) are the two factors that most effect alertness, performance, and rest / recovery. These two factors vary from individual to individual, and they also fluctuate within each individual during the phases of their lifetime. I don't want to bash getting up early. I have always believed that it is healthier to go to bed early and to get up earlier. But the fact is, getting enough quality sleep is a huge factor of elite performance.

Self-Discipline is <u>not externally enforced</u>. If your drill sergeant or parents or boss can get you to do something that you normally would not have the Discipline to do, then the behavior is there, but not the Discipline. <u>When you do the right thing because you want to, when no one is watching, then and only then have you developed true self-Discipline.</u>

Best Indicators Of

The best indicator of Discipline is <u>a lack of drama</u>. Again, this sounds odd. But hear me out. If you have the Discipline to make good decisions and to set boundaries with people who are not able to make good decisions, then your quality of life will be much higher. If you have the Discipline to walk away from an argument, it will not escalate into a fight. If you have the Discipline to study and work hard, then likely you are not going to be surrounded by knuckleheads and idiots whose lives are nothing but drama. I think we all know people who don't have the ability to hold back their temper. They escalate everything. They must be right, even if they are wrong.

Drama follows these people everywhere. They don't have the Discipline to hold back their passions.

Another indicator of Discipline is <u>order</u>. If you have the Discipline to establish and follow a process or system for the important aspects of your life, then you will have order. If you always put your keys in the same place when you get home, you will not have ten minutes of panic searching for them the next morning while you are running late for work. If you have the Discipline to file your papers and bills in an orderly manner, then you will not forget to pay a bill.

The final indicator of Discipline that I want to highlight is <u>health</u>. If you have the Discipline to not sabotage your body then you are going to be healthier. Junk food taste great. Chocolate and coffee, both made from beans, are my favorite vegetables. But the fact is, if you want to be healthy, you must have the Discipline to not smoke, significantly limit your alcohol consumption, and eat good, real food. If you want to be healthy, you must have the Discipline to work out a few times each week.

Too Much or Too Little

Too little Discipline, and you become a spoiled child who only takes the easy route. It is easier to get another credit card to buy stuff you don't need than it is to be disciplined and live in accordance with your budget. It is easier to eat junk food and drink soda than it is to be disciplined, plan your meals, and use your imagination to make delicious and healthy food. It is much easier to be a loser couch potato who spends all day watching your Smart TV and playing video games than it is to be disciplined and man-up.

Too much Discipline, and you become a robot. What enjoyment do you have in life if you are so disciplined that you never have fun, or relax, or sleep in, or eat the occasional piece of chocolate cake with ice cream?

Life is special. Enjoy it. But if you are disciplined about how and when you enjoy it … you will be able to enjoy more of it, and for a longer time.

Implications Of

If you are disciplined, then you are going to (1) perform better, (2) accomplish more, and (3) get in less trouble.

<u>Perform Better</u>: By having Discipline in your life, you will make better decisions in regard to your health, your education, your career, your friendships, your life. Rather than enjoying junk food, you will eat good food. Rather than being

lazy, you will have the Discipline to go to a hard school where you will learn more. Rather than doing the minimum like many work colleagues, you will have the Discipline to do the right thing and will get recognized and promoted. Rather than settling for who is available, you will have the Discipline to hold out for friends who are of the same caliber. Discipline will work itself into all aspects of your life, helping you to execute at a higher level.

Accomplish More: Someone who is disciplined will be more productive with their time and life and be able to get more done. If you get home from work and watch Netflix until midnight, you are wasting your precious life. But if you have the Discipline to not turn on the TV, you will for sure find the time to work out, do household chores, cook a healthy meal, invest in important relationships, read a few pages of a good book, and get a better night of sleep.

Get in Less Trouble: Everyone I know who is not disciplined gets in trouble. This goes for the jerks and also for the nice people. The passionate and undisciplined jerk is constantly arguing. He needs to be right. He needs to assert himself. The disciplined person doesn't "throw pearls before swine." They fight only the fights worth engaging in. They save their passion and energy for other, more important things. The nice, but undisciplined, person is always late. They get fired because they don't finish projects on time or arrive to work on time, or clean up after themselves. Having Discipline prevents a lot of headaches.

How It's Built

<u>Discipline is built through suffering hardship</u>. I don't want to be overly dramatic, but if you suffer hardships, then you are better able to put lesser sacrifices in perspective. If you have known real sacrifices in life, then minor things like setting your alarm to get up early enough to be fifteen minutes early to work is not a big deal. But if you are a spoiled brat and every second needs to be about you, then you don't want to waste one second extra being early for work. And this bad attitude will cause you to be frequently late for work, ultimately leading to you getting fired or never promoted.

<u>Discipline is developed by learning to see the underlying purpose or cause</u>. If you are smart enough to see the purpose behind an action, then you will more readily internalize it and adopt it as a habit. If you don't know why eating healthy is so much better for your heart and blood pressure, then you are going to feed on junk food and get fat.

<u>Discipline is built by appreciating what you have</u>. If you respect and appreciate what you have, you will take care of it. This applies to a bicycle, a car, a job, and your life and body. If you appreciate your wife, then you have the Discipline not to cheat on her or lust after other women. If you appreciate your job, then you have the Discipline to show up on time and work hard. If you appreciate your car, you have the Discipline to maintain it and keep it clean. If you appreciate your life, you have the Discipline to take care of your nutrition and health.

And finally, <u>Discipline is built through habit</u>. You might have the Discipline to not eat chocolate cake for the first week after your New Year's Resolution. But ultimately, you need to make healthy eating a Discipline that you maintain for all of your life, not just the first week of January. Gym memberships are always popular in January. But because of a lack of Discipline, they fizzle out by March. If you make it a habit, you no longer need to have amazing Discipline. It simply becomes something you do regularly.

Lifestyle – Not Resolutions

It is very popular these days to make and have New Year's Resolutions. But the Truth is, most people don't have the Commitment or Discipline to accomplish their resolution. This is where we need to focus on developing a disciplined lifestyle rather than simply making a New Year's Resolution.

Sleeping During a Tactical Mission

We all get tired and want to sleep. But when you are on a mission and need to pull security, you can't sleep. You must have the Discipline to stay awake to protect yourself and your team. You must have the Discipline to do what is best for the good of the mission. If you take the selfish and undisciplined route, you could get everyone killed. Discipline is essential for maintaining security in a war zone.

Staying Up Late

Imagine an employee who likes to stay up late watching TV. Sometimes she is so into "her series" that she stays awake hours later than she should. Then her head is so full of stimulation and blue light that she has a hard time falling asleep. Although she is not late to work that often, she always seems to arrive in a state of disarray. Enough is enough, and you fire her. Goodbye. Why waste time with an employee who doesn't have the Discipline to go to bed on time or manage her morning routine?

Disciplined Eating

Let's finish with a positive family example of Discipline. A young married couple is excited to begin their life together and want to make good decisions for their future. Although the wife is a great cook, before getting married, the husband lived off of junk food. Because he worked out, it never seemed important to him to learn about eating intelligently. Early in their marriage, they practice Discipline and integrate one another's good habits and forget the bad ones. They join a gym and work out together three times a week. The wife cooks nutritious food and the husband develops the habit of eating real and healthy food. Their Discipline helps them to enjoy healthier lives and they will, no doubt, pass these Disciplines to their children.

Individual Training / Development Plan: (PTREXAR)

Now is the point where you need to take a break from this book, sit down with a piece of paper, and make a plan on how you are going to train / develop the mindset of Discipline. Use the below questions to help you make your plan.

If you are going to skip this section, then please at least answer the first question: Where am I the least disciplined?

Plan:
- Where am I the least disciplined?
- How can I improve my Discipline in that area?
- List three things I can do to increase my Discipline:
    - #1:
    - #2:
    - #3:
- How do I plan to accomplish each of the above?
    - Training Tasks / Behaviors / Actions?
    - Frequency of Training?
    - Milestones / Phases?
- How or where or in what situations can I rehearse showing or displaying Discipline?
- What is the purpose of developing Discipline?
- What is my ultimate Goal / End-State regarding Discipline?
- How can I evaluate if my Discipline training is working?

Train: Go out there and get to work. Start today. Do what you planned (above) to do. Train like you fight. Don't make this easy on yourself. Make your training harder and more difficult, so that when it becomes time to execute your goal, you will be overly prepared.

Rehearse: Put yourself in situations where you will be able to demonstrate Discipline.

Execute: Execute that final display of Discipline for which you have been planning. Accomplish your goal.

Analyze: Assess if your Discipline has grown and developed. Analyze how effective your training plan was. What did you do wrong during this PTREXAR cycle? How can you improve next time?

Repeat: Now get out there and do the whole PTREXAR cycle again! Get even better!

6: Commitment

Let me tell you a story about a friend of mine from the university. His name is Patrick, a privileged but determined rich kid from outside of Richmond, Virginia. When Patrick reported in to Special Forces Assessment & Selection (SFAS), the Cadre didn't care about his real name. They simply gave him a roster number: Oscar-96 (O is for Officer and 96 meant he was the 96th man in alphabetical number).

O96 was not accustomed to hiking all day with a heavy rucksack. For the past three years, he was a logistics officer in a mechanized infantry regiment. He had a HMMWV and a driver. Although he loved to lift weights and was stronger than most, hiking all day was simply not his forte.

During the final event at Selection, O96 fell and broke his foot. Each step caused more and more pain. He had to stop. But if he did stop, he wouldn't finish this mandatory pass-fail event, and the previous weeks of pain would have all been for nothing. He would fail "Selection" and have to do everything all over again next year once he healed back up. This was his worse fear. He checked his foot. He was pretty sure that it was broken. But thankfully it was not a compound fracture where the bones were sticking out of the skin.

In true Patrick fashion, he put his wool sock back on, tried to stabilize his foot and ankle with duct tape, covered the entire mess with a second sock, and then jammed it all into his boot, which he tied as tightly as he could bear. As long as he walked slowly and only on his heel, the pain was bearable. He only had nine miles left to go.

"*I can make this*," he said out loud to himself as he picked up his rucksack and began hobbling off towards the finish line. Each step was a pain he hated to endure. And each mile was probably going to require another month of recovery. But steps turned into minutes, and minutes into miles. He kept going as fast as he could.

His heart sank when his watch alarm started beeping. Despite his best effort, he had missed the cut-off time for the forty-mile ruck march, just over one mile away from the finish line.

"*Better late and broken, than a quitter,*" he mumbled to himself over and over for the next thirty minutes.

There was no fanfare at the finish line. Just a Sergeant First Class standing alongside the dark, snow-covered road with a headlamp and a clipboard.

Looking down at the roster number sewn onto the cargo pockets of Patrick's camouflage pants, the Cadre Sergeant calmly said, "Oscar-96, you are twenty-two minutes late. Better luck next year. Down the road 200m is a five-ton truck pulling a trailer. Throw your ruck in the trailer and jump in the bed. We're leaving in an hour to go get the quitters, and then we will head back to base."

"Roger, Sergeant," replied Patrick as he moved towards the truck of shame.

Patrick spent the next hour freezing to death in the back of the five-ton. Of course, the top was off; Special Forces trainees hadn't yet earned the privilege of a tarp to protect them from the rain or wind. Then they spent a second hour driving up and down the final miles of the ruck march route, looking for quitters on the side of the road.

It was the crack of dawn when they got back to base. As the rejected candidates were unloaded and moved to the headquarters to be out-processed, Patrick asked the Cadre Sergeant with the clipboard if he could please see a doctor or medic. "I'm convinced that it is broken. I don't want to be a troublemaker, Sergeant. I just don't want to injure it more."

"Sure, let's check it out," replied the Sergeant with his typical hint of skepticism. After 18 months as a Cadre Sergeant, SFC Lynch had seen hundreds of men make hundreds of excuses for why they couldn't meet the standards.

Patrick grabbed his rucksack and hobbled after SFC Lynch into the aid station. A few minutes later, the doctor arrived in workout clothes with a big case of pillow hair.

The doctor removed the boot, the outer sock, and cut away the duct tape. Seeing that the bottom sock was soaked in blood and pus, the doctor put on a pair of surgical gloves before continuing.

"Okay, the blood and pus are from the blisters on your heels. Those will heal up in a week or two. They look much worse than they are. I'll clean them up in a few minutes."

"But your foot is broken for sure. It's jacked up. We'll x-ray it right now to see how bad it is. And then we are going to have to get you back to Bragg right away. I'm pretty sure that you are going to need surgery. How long did you walk funny with that blistered heel before you broke your foot?"

"Oh, no, Doc. My foot and skin and heel were fine. I fell and hurt my foot. I was pretty sure that it was broken, so I tried to brace it up as best I could with the duct tape and socks, and by tying my boot extra tight. I got those blisters trying to finish the forty-miler. Looks like it was all for nothing, now."

"How far back did you break your foot?"

"It was fifteen minutes after point four. So, I figure it was about nine miles."

"You're an idiot," interrupted the doctor, shaking his head. "You walked nine miles on a broken foot! You stupid SF guys are all the same. I just hope there isn't any permanent damage."

Five minutes later, Patrick was driving back to Fort Bragg with the doctor. Ninety minutes later, he was in surgery. The surgeons were able to put everything back in place and Patrick would be able to make a full recovery. After sleeping off and on for the next twenty-four hours, Patrick was surprised to see SFC Lynch, the Cadre Sergeant, walk into his hospital room.

"Oscar-96, glad to hear that your foot is going to make a full recovery. I just wanted to congratulate you on getting selected to begin Special Force training. You were a few minutes late for your forty miles. But since you hiked the last nine miles with a broken foot, we decided to make an exception. Your Commitment is exactly what are looking for. Well done."

Definition & Considerations

The definition of Commitment is "a <u>promise</u> or <u>firm decision</u> to do something"[6] <u>with follow-through</u> and no turning back.

We see this definition exemplified in my friend Patrick, O96, who was committed to finishing Special Forces Selection. He followed through and never turned back … even finishing the last fitness test with a broken foot.

Most dictionaries refer to Commitment as a <u>pledge or obligation</u>. For example, "We pledge to provide this many troops to the UN Mission in Africa." Or "I pledge to be there for you as your husband for the rest of my life."

But these definitions forget the most important part of the pledge or promise or obligation, <u>the follow-through.</u> Talk is cheap. Actions speak louder than words. It is easy to pledge more troops, more difficult to actually train and deploy troops. It is easy to pledge to be a good husband, but harder to follow through with actually being a good husband.

---

[6] https://dictionary.cambridge.org/dictionary/english/commitment

The last part of our definition involves <u>no turning back</u>. This is a matter of honor, but sometimes physics. A man of honor promises to love and cherish his wife as long as they both shall live. There is no turning back once you get married. Once a paratrooper jumps out the door of a C130 airplane, he is committed. There is no turning back and returning to base. He must land and finish his mission.

<u>Reliable</u>: We can't discuss Commitment without mentioning reliability. No one is reliable these days. The majority of people out there are late, flakey, and never do what they say. Reliability is 100% or nothing. You are either reliable or unreliable. While being reliable is black or white, there are shades of gray along the spectrum of unreliability. This spectrum runs from "unreliable" to not "usually reliable" to "fairly reliable" and ends with "usually reliable." The problem is that even someone who is "usually reliable" is sometimes flakey. And this means we can't count on them for something important. And this is why unreliable people are kicked out of Special Operations training and are never given the chance to get to a team. When the stakes are life and death, I never want to put my life in the hands of someone who is only "usually reliable." Only the reliable and committed make it to the teams.

<u>Willpower</u>: Many people have asked me about "how to have more willpower." I think willpower is the wrong word. Literally, willpower is "want" power. And this is inherent in all people. It is so easy for us to want something. Sometimes we want good things … such as health for our parents. Sometimes we want frivolous things… as in, I want to drive a Lamborghini. But for the most part, willpower is trying not to do something bad … as in, I don't have the willpower to eat healthy, so I have chocolate ice cream for dessert every night. Most SOF guys I know are compulsive. When they want something, they go get it. If they want ice cream for dessert, they get ice cream for dessert. If they want to get the new truck, they go buy one. So in this sense, I am going to say that SOF guys don't have willpower. But in the sense of following through with promises and accomplishing difficult things, SOF guys have a lot of Commitment and Discipline. And this is what people are asking about when they want to know how to have more willpower. What they really need is Commitment and Discipline. And for this reason, I am not going to discuss "willpower" as a separate mindset. I made it a paragraph in the chapter on Commitment here, after the chapter on Discipline.

What it isn't

A Commitment is not just making a promise.

A Commitment is not just making a pledge to do something.

A Commitment is not just making a firm decision to do something.

A Commitment is not just acknowledging your moral obligation to do something.

All of these false Commitments are easy to make. Perhaps they are done to save face, to be politically astute, to get accolades. A real Commitment, from a person of character, also involves the follow-through.

What it is

A Commitment is making a promise and following through with it.

A Commitment is making a pledge to do something and following through with it.

A Commitment is making a firm decision to do something and then following through with it.

A Commitment is acknowledging your moral obligation to do something and then following through with it.

Best Indicators Of

The best indicator of Commitment is when you never even consider quitting. Anything short of finishing is unacceptable. A committed father will never give up on his wife or kids. A committed Special Operations teammate will fight to the death to protect the brothers on his left and right. Quitting or walking away was never an option.

Your priorities are also indicators of your Commitment. If you are truly committed to finishing something, then you make it a priority. I've never met a MARSOC Raider who was in bad shape. I never met one who said, "I was too tired and unmotivated to work out." Never. They are all in great shape. And this is because they are committed to their community and would never give anything less than 100% to their physical training. If you are committed to your marriage, then you make it your priority. Your hobbies, video games, and buddies are not priority one. Your wife is priority one. You are committed to her and she is your priority.

Your time is another indicator of Commitment. If you are committed to doing something then you dedicate time to accomplishing it. If you don't care about something, it is much more difficult to commit the time required to accomplishing it.

Too Much or Too Little

Too much Commitment will result in <u>exhaustion</u>. You can't possibly commit to and finish everything of interest. You have to pick and choose where and when you will commit. And when you do, you follow it through to completion.

Too much Commitment will also result in <u>trouble</u>. It is impossible to be 100% all the time. Sometimes you just need to walk away. Passionate people are always letting their temper control their behavior. They get fired up and then they are all in, fully committed. They want to fight it out. And this leads to trouble. Better yet is the intelligent person who knows when to walk away from a situation to focus on more important matters.

Too little Commitment and you will always keep your options open. You will become <u>flakey</u>. People will stop respecting you, and your character will be as weak as your Commitment.

Too little Commitment will also result in a lot of promises and pledges, but no follow-through. This will destroy your reputation and cause honorable people to stop trusting you. An example of this is a politician who makes campaign promises and political pledges to get votes but who doesn't follow through.

Implications Of

If you are committed, you are going to (1) accomplish what you start, (2) have a better reputation, and (3) be a person of integrity.

<u>Accomplish What You Start</u>: If you are committed to what you promise, you will follow through with it until it is accomplished. You will only promise what you will be able to finish. And you will finish and do more in your life than those whose actions don't speak louder than words.

<u>Have a Better Reputation</u>: By completing what you finish, you will stand out. People will notice you. You will be seen and known as someone who is reliable. Your reputation will become exceptional.

<u>Integrity</u>: Nothing shows more integrity than doing what you say you are going to do. Don't just pledge or promise. Do it. Complete it. Follow through. In doing so, you will be able to hold your head up high as a person of integrity.

How It's Built

<u>Commitment is built by finishing what you start</u>. And you need to start young. If you learn early in life that it is okay to join a team but then quit halfway through the season, you will never learn Commitment before it counts. Of course, you

may be a late bloomer, but most flakey adults were flakey children whose parents enabled their flakiness. If you join a team, finish the season. If you make a promise, do it. If you pledge money, give it.

Commitment, in the sense of "pledge" or "promise," is built by knowing the limits of your abilities and <u>only letting your mouth pledge what your actions will back up</u>. Knowing your abilities and Competence (Chapter 3: Competence) will help you to only promise (Chapter 2: Truth) that with which you can follow through. If you know that you only have $100 dollars in the bank, you can only pledge $100 in support. If you know that you are a decent soccer player who wants to improve, then you can commit to being on the local team for the summer season. If you pledge and promise that which you don't have or are not capable of giving, then you are either dumb or a liar. I recommend that you watch what you say and promise. Only commit to doing what you can do.

Commitment is built by <u>taking ownership of your promises and pledges</u>. I'm not going to say that you are going to be successful at everything you commit to. But you should never give less than 100%. Sometimes you have to be so committed that you will die before failing. Most people don't have this much Commitment. But if you own your promise and will stop short of nothing less than completion, it is much easier to do what is required to do.

Commitment is built by <u>understanding the purpose of what you are doing</u>. A young kid quits his soccer team because it isn't fun. He doesn't realize that he is learning teamwork, developing foot-hand-eye coordination and agility, improving cardiovascular fitness, and building skills that will serve him well for a lifetime. If he knew all that he would or could learn from finishing the season, he might be less likely to grind his parent into allowing him to quit. Likewise, if you understand the purpose and the destination of your endeavors, it is much easier to see them through to completion.

Burn the Ships

Most of us know the legend of the Spanish Conquistador Hernán Cortés who conquered the Aztec Empire in the early part of the 16th century. Upon arriving to the New World, he had his men burn the ships. The message was clear. "We are here to stay. There is no going back."

Too many men and women these days keep their options open. They want to dabble in a bit of this and a bit of that. If they like it, cool. If not, they can try something else. But keeping your options open is not a good way to go through life. It produces flakey people who don't have the ability or Courage to commit.

I'm not saying that you need to "burn the ships" for everything that you do. That would be reckless and irresponsible. But there certainly are occasions when an absolute Commitment is needed. And in those situations, "burn the ships."

The Heroic CCT

I had the honor of working with a true hero, one who embodied Courage and Commitment. Bob was a member of the Air Force Special Operations Community, a Close Combat Technician (CCT) assigned to work with one of the Special Forces Teams in our Task Force. While on a critical mission to kill or capture an extremely dangerous arms dealer, bomb maker and flat-out criminal in western Afghanistan, his team hit heavy resistance and got into a huge battle.

Bob was shot in the chest. He could have given up. But he didn't. He was committed to surviving. He was committed to protecting his team and doing his job. His lung started filling up with blood. While the Special Forces medic provided life-saving treatment, Bob continued to engage the enemy with his rifle. Despite his injuries, despite not able to properly breathe, and despite being overwhelmed by enemy gunfire, Bob knew that Close Air Support (CAS) was the only way to save his team and that no one else on the team could call in CAS as well as he could. In between chest decompressions, Bob was able to call in three different CAS missions. His Competence (Chapter 3) as a Joint Tactical Air Controller (JTAC) enabled A-10 strafing runs to kill the enemy forces who were as close as thirty feet away. His Commitment to his team gave him the strength he needed to fight through the pain of his injury and the stress of the battle.

New Job / Start-Up

Starting a new job is difficult. Usually when starting a new job, a professional will work really hard to develop their Competence. Starting a new business is even more demanding. Not only do you have more work, you must also do all of the legal and administrative tasks associated with starting a new business. You must also take care of the practical and logistical aspects of renting or buying a work facility, making a network, paying your employees, and organizing offices. If a new job requires forty hours of max effort and performance each week, starting a business requires eighty.

Roughly twenty percent of businesses fail in their first year. Often this is because new business leaders significantly underestimated the amount of work it would take to see their business idea to fruition. When the workload continued to get greater and greater, they quit. They lacked Commitment.

If you have a business idea and are convinced that it is going to be a success, then go for it. But know this: you will need to be committed that first year (or two) to working like a dog to ensure that it succeeds.

Old-School Commitment

A young man and woman were delighted to meet each other and spend the entire afternoon together at a town event. They really liked each other. The next day, the young man went to her house and asked her father if he could have his blessing to marry his daughter. A month later, they were married. They stay married for sixty-two years before time and old age caught up with both of them. What a wonderful story of Commitment and love. And it was very common three generations ago … but absurd now a days.

Three generations ago, you could call out and kill a man for being dishonorable. Nowadays, most men don't have the slightest understanding of the concept of honor.

In a time where you live with your boyfriend or girlfriend for a few years before ever even discussing marriage, it seems ludicrous to make a lifelong Commitment to someone you barely know. But if you are a man or woman of integrity, and can commit to what you pledge, you can make any relationship work. Sadly, most people like to keep their options open. This goes for what to do on a Friday night, as well as upgrading their wife every five to ten years.

I recommend the old-fashioned ways. If you make a Commitment, follow it through to completion.

Individual Training / Development Plan: (PTREXAR)

Now is the point where you need to take a break from this book, sit down with a piece of paper, and make a plan on how you are going to train / develop the mindset of Commitment. Use the below questions to help you make your plan.

If you are going to skip this section, then please at least answer the first question: Where am I the least committed?

<u>Plan</u>:
- Where am I the least committed?

- How can I improve my Commitment in that area?
- List three things I can do to increase my Commitment:
    - # 1:
    - # 2:
    - # 3:
- How do I plan to accomplish each of the above?
    - Training Tasks / Behaviors / Actions?
    - Frequency of Training?
    - Milestones / Phases?
- How or where or in what situations can I rehearse showing or displaying Commitment?
- What is the purpose of developing Commitment?
- What is my ultimate Goal / End-State regarding Commitment?
- How can I evaluate if my Commitment training is working?

<u>Train</u>: Go out there and get to work. Start today. Do what you planned (above) to do. Train like you fight. Don't make this easy on yourself. Make your training harder and more difficult, so that when it becomes time to execute your goal, you will be overly prepared.

<u>Rehearse</u>: Put yourself in situations where you will be able to demonstrate Commitment.

<u>Execute</u>: Execute that final display of Commitment for which you have been planning. Accomplish your goal.

<u>Analyze</u>: Assess if your Commitment has grown and developed. Analyze how effective your training plan was. What did you do wrong during this PTREXAR cycle? How can you improve next time?

<u>Repeat</u>: Now get out there and do the whole PTREXAR cycle again! Get even better!

7: Motivation

I would like to introduce you to a hero of mine, a Special Force Medic named "Brandon." Brandon worked for me for a few months during my first deployment to Afghanistan. We were operating out of Kandahar and Brandon was sent up from his Special Forces Operational Detachment Alpha (ODA) to help his company get operations resourced and approved. Brandon was bright, sharp, and a lot of fun to work with. But he was an abysmal staff guy. I've seen elementary students with better computer skills than Brandon. He gave me 100% every day, but I frequently got mad at him because his computer skills were so bad and so slow. Although I really liked him as a person, I was so glad to see him rotate back to his team. His replacement was a computer nerd, ten times more effective as a staff guy.

What shocked me was that less than a week after getting back to his team, his ODA fell victim to a very complex and well-thought-through Taliban attack. Hundreds of Taliban fighters continued to arrive on the scene in waves and waves of counterattacks. Brandon had an injured teammate laying on the far side of a field, which was under fire by the Taliban. Brandon tried to low crawl through a small drainage ditch to reach his teammate. But his body armor was so full of gear that it stuck out from above the drainage ditch and was attracting enemy fire. So, he took off his body armor and low crawled 100m, while dragging his first aid bag, along the drainage ditch to provide emergency first aid to his injured colleague. Brandon treated his buddy, dragged him back into cover, and got him MEDEVACed to safety.

Two days later, Brandon and the rest of the team were pulled back to headquarters to refit and check in on their injured. I ran into Brandon, and in true SF fashion, he said to me: "You see, sir, I'm not a total screw-up. I'm much more reliable in the field than behind a desk."

Although Brandon was put in for the Medal of Honor, it was downgraded to a Silver Star. Nonetheless, Brandon is a true hero. He was a terrible staff member, but a dedicated member of the team who was motivated to go above and beyond the call of duty to care for and save his brothers.

Definition & Considerations

Let's define Motivation as the **reason** to do something, **willingness** to do something, and / or **enthusiasm** to do something.[7] Reason is your

---

[7] https://dictionary.cambridge.org/dictionary/english/motivation

purpose. Willingness is a measurement of Commitment. And enthusiasm is emotional, a result of passion, caring, or enjoyment.

But with that said, there are thousands of nuances for Motivation, Motivation theory, and willpower. In true "Life is a Special Operation" fashion, let's throw most of that philosophical and academic fluff out the window and get to the heart of the matter: What motivates Special Operation Forces to endure some of the hardest and most difficult training in the world, and how do they sustain that Motivation throughout a career of dangerous and demanding missions and deployments? And what can we learn from it?

I'm going to assert that there is not a Motivation difference between enduring training and "driving on to the Ranger objective, though I be the lone survivor."[8] Behavior for preparing for and enduring training is a bit different from behavior during dangerous missions. But the Motivation is the same. Let's look at some other motivational considerations.

<u>Reason / Purpose</u>: It is very important to know the reason you are doing something. If you know and have taken ownership of the purpose for your

---

[8] The Ranger Creed

mission, you will almost always succeed. Imagine you are a candidate in the PJ (U.S. Air Force Pararescue) training pipeline. You have always wanted to be in the Air Force so you can do Special Ops "Search and Rescue" so "that others may live." You know that being on a PJ team is going to be worth any sacrifice you have to make to endure training. You understand your purpose for enduring training and are much more likely to be motivated to give 100% every day.

Tribal Motivation: One of the most important motivational factors is the fear of letting down your tribe. Just as I would hate to let down my family and would rather die than let down my wife, when I was in the Army, I never wanted to let down my tribe. I remember doing a full-day fitness competition when I was in the 101st Airborne Division as a young Lieutenant. I was placed on a team with three other 1st Lieutenants, my friends, who just happened to be amazing athletes. I recognized immediately that I was on the winning team, and that I was the weakest link. I didn't want to let my buddies down, and so I dug deep, and gave 100%. Because of my willingness to not let down my friends, I made a personal best time on a twelve-mile road march. Never once in the thousands of miles I have hiked and rucked since then have I ever been as fast as that ruck march. I was motivated to support the tribe.

I think we all have read an article or seen an interview where a soldier does something heroic in a warzone and they say, "I did it for my buddies on my left and right." Let me put that another way: "I was motivated by my Commitment to my tribe to do heroic actions in order to protect the men on my left and right." <u>Never underestimate the power of belonging</u>. This tribal Motivation has two phases. The first is getting accepted. "I am motivated to prepare for and endure hard training so I can become a member of that elite tribe." The second is belonging. "I am a member of an elite tribe, and I will do everything possible to protect and provide for this team."

<u>Motivation through Pride</u>: The implications of Motivation by pride are twofold: One is the <u>fear of failure</u>. Another is the drive to <u>be the best</u>. I think they are both closely related and a very important subset of the Special Operations Mindset.

When I was in the Special Forces course, we had a phase of training called the (Military Occupational Specialty) "MOS phase." During this phase all MOSs were separated for technical training. Communications specialists studied how to use computers and radios. Medics went off together to learn medical and emergency trauma skills. Engineers went to engineering school. Weapons sergeants went to study weapons. And officers studied tactics and leadership, mastered the military planning processes, and learned Special Operations-specific skills and competencies. I have to admit that the group dynamics of this phase were exceptional. It is rare to put so many intelligent and driven alpha males into such close proximity. We would study a subject and then go into the woods for a Field Training Exercise (FTX) for a few days to do it. The training scenarios during every FTX were orchestrated so that inevitably something would fail or go wrong. And when it did, we would beat ourselves up and internalize the lesson learned to the point that we would never repeat the mistakes that we made during the training exercise. Looking back, I consider it a couple of months of "learning by failure." I was so motivated to be a success and to be number one, that every failure was a catastrophic event. Every failure was because as an officer and leader, I didn't do something correctly, or I didn't think of something essential, or I failed to prepare or plan for a contingency.

Special Operators are more critical of themselves than anyone else. They suffer when they fail and make sure that they will never fail again. If you have a motivated team, then be assured that they will learn more from a failure than from a success. Pride (fear of failure and the desire to be the best) is an important factor of human Motivation and an ever-present characteristic of the Special Operations Mindset.

<u>Motivation is individual</u>. Special Operators are self-motivated. No one has to tell them to work out, to train hard, to learn and master their craft. No one has to wake them up and remind them to go to school. They have their purpose and reason. They would never want to do or give anything less that their best (pride in their individual excellence), and under no circumstances would they ever let down their tribe.

<u>Motivation is also social.</u> Every Raider on a Marine Special Operations Team (MARSOT) pushes himself every day to get stronger and faster. This is because the team and community value physical fitness and Readiness. The individual is motivated to be physically fit because collectively, the community values fitness. Likewise, civilian team and business members will often be motivated by that which motivates their entire team and business. If everyone at work has an iPhone, then you are more likely to trade in your Android phone for an iPhone. If everyone in your family is industrious and values hard work, then you are more likely to be industrious and hardworking. The implication of social Motivation is that you will generally adapt to the collective. So if you want to be excellent, you better hang around with people who are also

seeking and working towards excellence. If your friends and colleagues and family are not committed to excellence, you better break away from them before they hinder your Motivation to perform.

Motivation through Control: We are much more likely to be motivated to do something if we believe that we can control the outcome. If we believe that our efforts and skills and input and Commitment with affect the outcome, then we are much more likely to be motivated to accomplish difficult things. But if you don't think that you will be able to control the outcome, you are significantly less likely to be motivated to try. The implication here is that Special Operators believe their efforts will always have an impact on the results. And so, they are much more likely to go through hard training and to accomplish difficult missions.

Willpower: Willpower is a muscle. If you use it, it will get stronger. If you never use it, it will be a weak muscle and you will be a weak person, dare I say loser. The problem with willpower in a chapter on Motivation is that willpower is how not to do a negative behavior, while Motivation in this book is how to do difficult but positive behaviors. A negative behavior is drinking too much beer, smoking, staying up too late, eating too much junk food, playing too many video games, watching porn, having an affair. Positive behaviors are staying healthy, getting into amazing shape, enduring difficult training, becoming competent and mastering your craft, taking Responsibility for your life, making the world a better place, and being the best of the best, day in and day out, year after year.

I hate to focus too much on negative behaviors. But for sure, I will share with you my radical opinion. If you don't have the willpower to stop negative behaviors, then we don't want you in the Special Operations community. You are prone to become loser. A man who can't control himself enough to stop a negative behavior will never have the Motivation to be the best of the best. So, if you were hoping for something more politically correct, then go back to the top of this paragraph. Start exercising your willpower muscles with something small, and continue to build those muscles until they are strong.

Self-Fulfilling Prophecy: One man says he can do it. Another says he can't do it. Both are right. It is important to be honest with yourself, to be realistic about your abilities and competencies. But it is also important to be positive. You might not be able to accomplish something now. But with training and development, you may be able to accomplish it next year. I include self-fulfilling prophecy under Motivation because if you want something bad enough, and are positive about your ability to achieve it, you are much more likely to be able to accomplish your goal.

<u>Motivation through Confidence</u>. The more confident you are that you can do something, the more likely you will do it. This is a variation of the self-fulfilling prophecy ... but one which presumes that Confidence comes from accomplishing hard things and is a result of a Competence based upon knowledge and skill.

<u>Motivation through Identity</u>: If you link a challenge to your identity, you will be able to do it. If you link a challenge to a negative activity, you will fail. The easiest example is eating junk food. If you are motivated to be healthy, you will say to yourself, "I am a healthy person. I don't eat junk food." And you are less likely to eat junk food. But if you say to yourself, "It is so terrible that I can't eat junk food," you will always crave it and eventually give in to your appetite.

If you look at a challenge as a negative task, then you will never accomplish it. "Everyone says Ranger School sucks, what a pity that I have to go to that school." This is a negative attitude and will unlikely result in a motivated Ranger student. But if you link the challenge to your identity, you will be much more motivated to accomplish Ranger School. "I am a professional and competent warrior. No school is too hard for me, and I want to learn everything I can before I deploy." This type of attitude will be successful.

<u>Enthusiasm</u>. If you have fun or enjoy or want to do something, you are much more likely to be motivated to do it. As we discussed earlier in the chapter on Commitment, an honorable man who makes a pledge will complete it, whether difficult or easy. But if you are enthusiastic about doing it or enjoy doing it, then it is significantly easier for you to complete your pledge. You will be more motivated to complete your pledge. And this leads us to "doing what you want to do."

Do What You Want to Do

This is one of my favorite pieces of advice. I have written about this concept several times and have even made a YouTube video about it. It has to do with being enthusiastic about your occupation so you will always remain motivated to do it.

Because of the prestige associated with elite occupations, many people want to be a doctor, a lawyer, or a Special Forces Green Beret. But when it is time to get to work, these people don't want to do what doctors do, what lawyers do, or what Special Forces Green Berets do.

For example, many people tell me they want to be a lawyer. I tell them: "Great. So, you love to spend eighteen hours a day in a research library reading over case files. You want to micromanage your time so that you bill every six-minute increment to a different client. You want to work hard and be the brightest because justice in this world doesn't exist, and usually the best-prepared lawyer is the one who wins. If that is what you want to do, then go for it. But if you simply just want to be a lawyer, then you will flunk out of the first year of law school."

Many people tell me they want to be a Green Beret. I then tell them: "Great. So, you want to train so hard that by the time you are forty, your body is completely broken. You want to spend six months of every year away from your wife and kids in a smelly Third-World country chasing the worst bad guys on Earth and watching 25% of your best friends get killed or injured. You want to wear your thirty-pound body armor and Kevlar helmet so much that you don't even notice that they are on. Because this is what Green Berets do."

It is important to do what you want to do. "Being" something will eventually cause you to lose Motivation and fail. But if you are doing what you want to do, then you will be more enthusiastic and motivated to do something.

What it is

<u>Motivation is action</u>. If you are unmotivated to do something, you will not do it or you will do it reluctantly. But if you are motivated to do something, you do it. So, in this sense, Motivation is always manifested in action. If you are motivated to be healthy, then you will make good decisions, work out, and eat healthy. If you are motivated to be the best employee in a company, then you will work hard, learn policy, and volunteer for opportunities to learn and develop.

What it isn't

<u>Motivation isn't false</u>. As a young ROTC Cadet at Fort Benning, I was very impressed with the "Black Hats" (Instructors) at Airborne School. They were loud and confident. I can still remember them yelling, "Are you motivated?" Then hundreds of Airborne students would simultaneously reply, "We are motivated, motivated, motivated, Sergeant. Airborne!" It was all big fun and games at eighteen years old. But that isn't real leadership and Motivation. Being loud and dynamic and confident works for simple things, easy things. But it doesn't work when you are really suffering, when you are digging so deep to finish strong that you hardly have anything left. Pretending to be excited might get you through a four-mile run singing cadences about jumping

out of airplanes. But for sure it won't work during a forty-mile hike in the rain with an eighty-pound rucksack.

<u>Motivation isn't borrowed</u>: Let's say that your best friend wants to be a Navy SEAL. He talks you into joining the Navy, and you both go off to training. It has always been his dream to be a SEAL, and so he is motivated to succeed. You, on the other hand, are motivated to be a supportive friend, not to endure Navy SEAL training. He may succeed. But you will fail.

Best Indicators Of

The best indicator of Motivation is <u>action</u>. If you are motivated to do something, then you will do it. Talk is cheap. Your actions speak louder than words. So, if you are motivated to do or accomplish something, do it.

Another indicator of Motivation is <u>self-starting</u>: If you are motivated to do something, then you are going to be a self-starter. No one needs to remind you to work out if you are motivated to get into amazing shape. No one needs to remind you to study if you are motivated to get straight As and graduate with honors.

Motivated people find <u>enjoyment</u> in what they are doing. If you are motivated to do something, then it is likely that you have internalized your purpose and reason for doing it. In most cases, you will then do it more willingly. I think ruck marching is such a great example. If you are motivated to pass Special Operations training, then you will find enjoyment in ruck marching. Not because ruck marching in and of itself is enjoyable. But because you know that being in SOF means that you must be prepared to carry your field gear, or your body armor and kit in an urban situation, on your back for long times and long distances. If you are motivated to be a pianist, then you want to practice and know how important it is. You will enjoy practicing, and you will improve much more quickly than a child whose parents are making them take piano lessons.

Too Much or Too Little

Too much Motivation, and you could really wear yourself out. This is a passionate artist who is inspired to work on his masterpiece all night.

Too little, and you need a kick in the butt to do anything and everything. "Get out of bed, you lazy kid." "Do your homework." "Did you go to the gym this week?" If you are not motivated to do something, you will never do it.

SOF don't need someone to yell at them to motivate them. There is no cheering at the top of the mountain. Motivated people simply do it because they know that what they are doing is worth the effort.

Implications Of

If you are motivated, then you are going to (1) perform better, and (2) accomplish more.

<u>Perform Better</u>: A motivated person will enjoy what they are doing. They will take more ownership of it. They will do it and will likely do it better than someone who doesn't care about it or is not motivated.

<u>Accomplish More</u>: Doers do. Lazy people waste their life being entertained. If you are motivated to accomplish or do one thing, that will likely lead you to accomplish or do another, then another. This is why successful people are successful again and again. Rarely do you see a successful person retire or stop after one accomplishment. Their hard work is positively reinforced through their success, and so they are more motivated to keep going.

How It's Built

<u>Motivation is built by knowing your purpose / reason</u>. It can come in an instant … and that is why people are motivated to do heroic things like jumping on a grenade or jumping into the river to save a drowning child. But it can also be studied, learned, calculated … as in, "I want to be a part of this community and so any physically difficult training will be worth the effort and sacrifice I make to endure training."

Motivation is <u>built through identity</u>. If your identity is associated with a certain tribe, then you will be motivated to work to protect or to provide for that tribe. If your identity is associated with your faith, then you will be motivated to act and behave in accordance with your faith. If your identity is associated with a characteristic, for example health, then you will be more motivated to display characteristics that exemplify health. The stronger your identity is associated with a characteristic, tribe, or faith, the more motivated you will be to act in accordance with your beliefs or for the good of your team.

Business Motivation

I want to talk about my business plan for Life is a Special Operation. When I started my YouTube channel, I wanted to help people achieve their dreams and to inspire the next generation of leaders. Looking at the YouTube algorithm, I would have had five times more subscribers and views if I showed my face. It is so much easier to relate to a person and face than a voice and wisdom. But I valued privacy and didn't want to be famous. Being famous is complicated. I enjoy my life and want to have my peace and privacy.

The other way I could have significantly boosted my YouTube performance would have been by putting half-naked women on my video thumbnails and in my videos. But I am a professional. I value and respect women and don't want to sellout my dignity by using the technique of "sex sells." And knowing this, I still started my YouTube channel anyways. And yet it did grow, albeit slower than so many other channels.

The reason it kept growing and keeps growing is because I work very hard every day for this channel. I am motivated to help educate and inspire the next generation of leaders. My Motivation keeps me up late at night typing the text for another video. My Motivation gets me up in the morning to edit the next video. I knew it would be extra work, but I was and am motivated to make a difference.

Selfishly Motivated Appeasement

Let's talk about Motivation by using a negative example. Two people are selfish and motivated by their own happiness. They think being married will fill a gap in their lives and make them happier. So, they married. A year later, the happiness wears off. They then decide that a baby might make them happier.

They realize too late that their baby is a lot of work. They miss the days when they could stay up late, be more spontaneous, and hang out with their single friends. Rather than being motivated to love, care for, develop, and nurture their kid, their focus is on what they are not able to do since having the baby.

Rather than teaching the baby to be self-entertaining, to not throw tantrums, that he must eat what they give him, and that the world doesn't revolve around his happiness and entertainment, they are motivated to appease him. If the baby isn't crying, then they have their peace and can focus on their own entertainment and happiness. Their Motivation is selfish. They want the baby appeased so they can have their peace. But now the baby rules the family. They only eat where the kid wants to eat. The kid watches hours of his favorite videos each night before going to bed. The kid joins every team he sees and quits a few weeks later. Rather than being motivated to develop an intelligent and capable kid, the parents were selfishly motivated to appease him so they can have their peace. They created a below-average child who will never be self-sufficient.

Hell Week

I want to give you a training vignette from the life of a Navy SEAL who I had the honor of working with at Special Operations Command–Europe. His name is Mark, a college football star and the father of two bright and beautiful young girls. Mark's story begins halfway through Hell Week. He hasn't slept in days and is running on adrenaline and Motivation. He knows that he has less than forty-eight hours left until the pain is over. But forty-eight hours is a long time when every single minute is spent in a borderline state of hypothermic exhaustion.

It is night out, and the cadre just announced that they are going to do a surface swim in the freezing cold Pacific Ocean. As he sprints towards the surf, he is aware of how fatigued his muscles are and how the sand ruthlessly scratches away at the bleeding rash he has between his legs. He isn't sure what was worse, the temperature shock from diving headfirst into the oncoming wave or the sting of the saltwater as it exacerbates his rash.

For the next thirty minutes, he swims along the coast towards the turnaround point. Although he is more than aware of his pain and fatigue, he doesn't hesitate. He just gives his all, which is about 500% more than he thought it was a few months ago. He knows that any effort that he has to make to endure training will be worth the payoff of finally joining the elite Navy SEAL community.

His brain wanders to a potential scenario where his team is exhausted from a day-long firefight and they have to jump into ice cold water in the middle of the night to swim into open waters to meet their exfil boat for extraction. He now better understands the purpose for this torturous training. He realizes that he would only want men on his left and right upon whom he can rely. Men who don't know what quitting is. Men who are motivated to give and do whatever it takes to accomplish the mission.

Mark picks up his pace, partially because he is motivated to do well, and partially because the harder he swims, the warmer he gets. Nothing can stop him, now. Forty-seven more hours. Bring it on.

Individual Training / Development Plan: (PTREXAR)

Now is the point where you need to take a break from this book, sit down with a piece of paper, and make a plan on how you are going to train / develop the mindset of Motivation. Use the below questions to help you make your plan.

If you are going to skip this section, then please at least answer the first question: Where am I the least motivated?

Plan:
- Where am I the least motivated?
- How can I improve my Motivation in that area?
- List three things I can do to increase my Motivation:
    - # 1:
    - # 2:
    - # 3:
- How do I plan to accomplish each of the above?
    - Training Tasks / Behaviors / Actions?
    - Frequency of Training?
    - Milestones / Phases?

- How or where or in what situations can I rehearse showing or displaying Motivation?
- What is the purpose of developing Motivation?
- What is my ultimate Goal / End-State regarding Motivation?
- How can I evaluate if my Motivation training is working?

<u>Train</u>: Go out there and get to work. Start today. Do what you planned (above) to do. Train like you fight. Don't make this easy on yourself. Make your training harder and more difficult, so that when it becomes time to execute your goal, you will be overly prepared.

<u>Rehearse</u>: Put yourself in situations where you will be able to demonstrate Motivation.

<u>Execute</u>: Execute that final display of Motivation for which you have been planning. Accomplish your goal.

<u>Analyze</u>: Assess if your Motivation has grown and developed. Analyze how effective your training plan was. What did you do wrong during this PTREXAR cycle? How can you improve next time?

<u>Repeat</u>: Now get out there and do the whole PTREXAR cycle again! Get even better!

8: Responsibility

I want to tell you a tragic story about a friend of mine named Ronald, a fellow Ranger-qualified Special Forces Captain, who was in command of a special mission team in Kabul, the capital of Afghanistan. He and his team grew beards, wore civilian clothes, and worked with several different task forces and governmental agencies in our common fight against terrorism.

Coming back to his secure team house after a few days "down range," Ronald threw his clothes into the laundry basket, showered up, and took a quick nap before he began his report to higher headquarters. As he began to type up his report, his heart sank as he realized that he didn't have his thumb drive memory stick hanging around his neck on a piece of green 550 cord. He must have left it in his pants pocket when he got back from the mission. He ran to check out his dirty clothes basket, but it was empty. His Afghan maid must have picked up his laundry while he was napping.

After spending the next few hours trying to track down the maid, it became evident that she had grabbed it and ran away. Ronald reluctantly informed his higher headquarters of the massive intelligence breach. The entire intelligence and Special Operations community went on high alert. Finding this thumb drive and preventing it from falling into the hands of the bad guys was now priority one.

The next afternoon, a British intel team found a black memory stick on a green 550 cord necklace for sale at their local bazaar. The vendor did not know what it was, but he reluctantly let it go after bartering for an agreed-upon price, the equivalent of 25 U.S. dollars.

An analysis of the memory stick revealed that no one had attempted to unencrypt its contents and that it had not even been plugged into another computer at all. There were sighs of relief all throughout Afghanistan.

When Ronald arrived to the Combined Joint Special Operations Task Force – Afghanistan (CJSOTF-A) Headquarters to pick his memory stick back up, he was ushered in to see the Commander, who wanted to know what happened.

Ronald confidently walked into the Colonel's office and noticed right away that the Command Sergeant Major (CSM) was also in the room, holding his recovered thumb drive. Ronald reminded the Colonel and CSM how successful he and his team had been in the past months and took the opportunity to reiterate that they were under-manned and under-resourced for such an important mission. He then explained how shocked he was that his maid stole from him.

The Colonel asked him to shut the door.

"Ronald, I'm very disappointed in you," began the Colonel. "Last time I checked, Ranger School and the Q Course teach you that security is rule number one. I don't give a damn that your maid stole your memory stick. We are in a war, not the Hilton. Do your own laundry. You should have assumed that every person in the world wants to kill you for the info on that thumb drive. I can only imagine what would have happened if that information would have gotten into the wrong hands. It would have been absolutely catastrophic."

"And now you arrogantly prance into my office and blamed a high Operations Tempo (OPTEMPO), a lack of manning, a lack of resources, and a local national who had no reason for being in your team house. But you never thought of blaming yourself. You put comfort and rest above security. You're the type of cool guy that gives Special Forces a bad name."

"You're done. I'm firing you right now. You are relieved of your command. If you would have taken Responsibility for this situation, I might have been lenient. But you refused to man up to your mistake. Pack your bags. I want you out of Afghanistan on the next flight."

Definition & Considerations

Although there are many definitions of Responsibility to include "the quality or state of being responsible: such as (a) moral, legal, or mental accountability, (b) reliability, trustworthiness,"[9] I like the Cambridge Dictionary's definition the most: "something that it is your job or duty to deal with."[10] I appreciate that the definition includes "job or duty" as well as the expression "deal with" … as in "deal with it."

If you are the director of customer relations, then your "job or duty" is to manage how your business treats your customers. If there is a problem, you "deal with it." It doesn't matter if you are an introvert or an extrovert, or if someone else should have answered the phone. Your job is to manage your customers, and you better not shirk your responsibilities.

If you are the father of a child, then your "job or duty" is to provide for and raise that kid. If there is a problem, you "deal with it." It doesn't matter

---

[9] https://www.merriam-webster.com/dictionary/responsibility

[10] https://dictionary.cambridge.org/dictionary/english/responsibility

if the kid was planned, or you are also busy at work. If you think that you are man enough to make kids, then you better man up to your responsibilities. I can't tell you how much of my time has been wasted over the years dealing with stupid people. If only these idiots would have had parents who took Responsibility for their upbringing. Perhaps they would know basic math, how to budget, how to save, and how to work in a group or on a team. Forgive my justified tirade. But I blame lazy parents who appeased their kids instead of taking the Responsibility to engage, educate, and raise them properly.

<u>Leaders Give Praise but Take Fault</u>: If you are a leader of integrity, who takes Responsibility for everything that happens or fails to happen, then you are going to give praise, but take fault. If something goes correctly, you give the praise to the hard work of your team. If your team fails or makes a mistake, you take Responsibility for the fault.

What it is

<u>Responsibility is doing your duty</u>. If you are in charge of something or in control of something, then it is your duty to do it. A policeman is in charge of enforcing laws and protecting its citizens from injustice. A teacher must teach. A soldier must protect.

Responsibility is <u>being accountable</u>. When you sign your name onto a contract, it used to be that you are accountable for coming through with your terms of the agreement. Not anymore. You can simply not uphold your end of the bargain. Or you can get a lawyer who will gladly work on your behalf, for a large sum of money, to make you unaccountable for that which you deliberately signed that you would be accountable.

Responsibility is <u>being reliable</u>. If you say you are going to do something, then you do it. If you say you are going to be somewhere, you show up on time. This is a variation of Truth and Commitment. No one needs a flakey friend or teammate. Unreliable people are the weakest link on a chain, and they must be cut away.

Responsibility is <u>ownership</u>. Responsibility is taking ownership of your environment, family, team … everything within your span of control. I feel obligated to reference Jocko Willink & Leif Babin's bestselling book *"Extreme Ownership: How U.S. Navy SEALs Lead."*[11] This is an amazing book which dives into the theme of taking Responsibility.

---

[11] Published by St Martin's Press, 2017, ISBN 978-1250183866

What it isn't

<u>Responsibility is not keeping silent</u>. Perhaps you have heard the expression, "Admit to nothing, deny everything, and make counter-allegations?" It is silly and fun. But the fact is, only losers and criminals do this. If you are a man or woman of integrity, then you take Responsibility for everything within your circle of influence.

Responsibility is <u>not deferred</u>. When I was an undergrad, I read a case study about a woman being raped in the alley of a big city residential neighborhood. As the woman was screaming for help, a dozen people heard her pleas. But no one called the police or went downstairs to intervene or rescue the woman. After she was raped, she reported it to the local police department, and they conducted an investigation. During this investigation they found that twelve people in the neighboring apartment buildings heard the woman scream for help. But they all assumed that someone else would call the police. This is called "deferred Responsibility." No one took Responsibility for the situation of an innocent woman screaming for help in the back alley, and sadly, no one called for help.

Responsibility is <u>not giving excuses</u>: Have you ever noticed that some people always have an excuse for everything? Nothing is their fault. They are always right, never wrong. They're perfect. I'm so disgusted with people who refuse to take Responsibility for their actions. Let's looks at a few common excuses and see what the Truth is.

> "I'm late because of traffic." - No, you weren't late because of traffic. You are habitually late because you are too lazy to get up and leave twenty minutes earlier to mitigate heavy traffic.

> "My stupid alarm didn't go off." - No, your alarm isn't stupid. You are stupid. You know that you stay up late watching mind-numbing stuff on YouTube and TV and should have set one, two, or three alarms. Better yet, go to bed earlier.

> "We didn't finish the project on time because we didn't have enough budget." - Yes, the budget was lower than hoped for, but you have known about this limitation for months and yet you never found ways to overcome this challenge.

> "I'm slightly overweight because healthy food is so expensive." - No, you are overweight because you either don't know the importance of healthy eating or you do, but are undisciplined or too lazy to cook for yourself.

"I didn't finish training because the cadre was out to get me." - No, the cadre are not out to get you. You didn't get selected because you are selfish and not pulling your share of the weight.

By the time you're an adult, your life is your fault. Stop making excuses.

Responsibility is <u>not delegated</u>: Yes, delegation is good. But some things are your Responsibility, and your Responsibility alone. The boss is responsible for the company. The commander is responsible for the unit. The pilot is responsible for the plane. The father is responsible for the family. The captain is responsible for the ship. Don't shirk your responsibilities under the ruse of "delegating it to someone else." And for sure, never delegate the essential tasks.

Responsibility is <u>not being flakey</u>. We all know flakey people who arrive late, if they ever arrive at all. And then they have an excuse. You ask them to do something, and perhaps it gets done. I hope you only know people like this, but don't call them your friends. Set boundaries with flakey people. If they fail you for an appointment for a cup of coffee at the local café, they will fail you when life gets hard and you really need some help.

Best Indicators Of

<u>The best indicator of Responsibility is trust</u>. If you are responsible, people will trust you. Trust plays out in how people approach you for help and how they use you for work. Let me explain in greater detail.

People <u>bring their problems</u> to those they trust. If someone brings their problem to you for help, they are saying that they trust you to help them. They see you as someone who takes Responsibility and gets things done. If no one asks for your help, you might want to reconsider how people perceive you and your level of concern and abilities.

Another indicator of Responsibility is that <u>you keep getting more and more work</u>. We see this in every field. The reliable and trusted employee becomes the "go-to guy." Since he is responsible and reliable, we can assume that he will get it done. If this is you, then make sure that you are setting boundaries for yourself so that you don't become the "sucker," the guy who does most of the work for the team while the other members stand on the sidelines and watch. If you are a leader in this scenario, then please protect your "go-to guys." Let them do their work and be sure to develop them into more capable leaders and workers. But don't let them become the work horse behind all projects. This is a certain way to push them into burnout or to drive them to another company or team.

Too Much or Too Little

If you take too much Responsibility, then you become the "sucker," or the "martyr." This is the strong and hardworking dad who loves and takes Responsibility for his family and household. Rather than interrupting his daughter from her second hour of social media time, after he finishes his second job, he comes home and checks the windshield washer fluid level, takes out the trash, feeds the cat, empties the dishwasher, and changes lightbulbs. He is the sucker. All of these things his teenage daughter could have done, but out of love, he thinks he is doing her a favor. But he isn't. He is feeding her laziness.

Another example of this are the helicopter parents who are slaves to entertaining their children. Does she have the latest toy? Is his TV big enough? Does he like Cub Scouts or should he join karate? Can she do the rock band, and swim team, and church camp this summer? Rather than just telling the kids to read a book and entertain themselves, the parents have become a slave to their happiness, another "mother" or "father of the year" martyr.

If you take too little Responsibility, then you become flakey, unreliable. This is the other extreme of parents, those who have kids but who don't care about them or help develop them. Someone with too little Responsibility makes excuses for everything. They are late, but it is someone else's fault. They are not proficient, but it is someone else's fault. They are in debt because they seemingly "deserve" something they can't afford and never learned the habits of waiting and saving.

Implications Of

If you are responsible then you are going to (1) be trusted, (2) respected, and (3) relied upon.

Trusted: Responsible people are always trusted to help solve problems. If you have something important to solve or figure out, you never take it to your selfish and flakey acquaintances. You bring it to your most trusted and responsible friend or family member.

Respected: We respect those who take Responsibility more than those who make excuses. Even if you are not as successful as you would have dreamed yourself to be, we always respect those who "man up" or "woman up," do their duties, and deal with it.

Life is a Special Operation · 139

Relied Upon: Responsible people are always relied upon to get the job done. They are the "go-to guy." They don't shirk Responsibility or find excuses. They work hard and do their duty. They get it done.

How It's Built

Responsibility is built through trial and error, success and failures. If you do something well and succeed or win, develop your character and sense of Responsibility by giving credit to your colleagues or teammates. If you do something poorly or make mistakes, develop your character by assuming Responsibility for the failure, and commit to learning the lesson and never repeating it. As time goes by, you learn that when you take Responsibility for your failures and pass on credit for your successes, your supervisors will not get angry. On the contrary, they will see that you are not a "show-off" who points fingers for failure and takes credit for success. They will see that you are a team player, someone with depth of character.

Responsibility is built by doing your duty. If you are a member of the family, then do your share of the housework and keep your spaces clean and organized. If your parents buy you a vehicle, then take Responsibility for it by doing routine maintenance, keeping it clean, and driving it respectfully and intentionally. If you are a member of a team, then do your share and ask to help or do more when you have free time.

Responsibility is built by only blaming yourself. If you are not happy with who you are and where you are in life, take Responsibility for it and do what needs to be done to fix it. If there is a family dynamic that you don't like, take Responsibility for it and do what needs to be done to fix it. If your team's work at the office is sub-standard, take Responsibility for it and do what needs to be done to fix it.

Irresponsible Drinking

I feel obligated to tell you a terrible story of a Green Beret who worked for me who wasn't responsible for his behavior and spent ten years paying for it. After a standard weekday evening with a "Q Course buddy" at the local pub, a newly graduated Green Beret Sergeant by the name of Justin jumped into his 1990 Ford Bronco to drive home. He woke up in jail, unable to remember anything.

The Company Sergeant Major coordinated with the Fayetteville Police for Justin's release into military custody and drove him to my office where I, as his Company Commander, had the

Responsibility of explaining to him what happened. Being a Special Forces Company Commander was one of the highlights of my entire life. But that day, in particular, was one of my worst days in command.

I explained to him that while driving home last night, he ran full speed into the back of a car that was stopped at a traffic light. Police estimated that he was going sixty miles per hour when he rear-ended a teenage girl on her way home after dinner at a friend's house. She died instantly. Her car looked like it was hit by a train. The police at the scene of the crime found Justin sleeping soundly in the front of his Bronco, without a bruise or a scratch. The police arrested Justin and drove him to the jail, where he consented to a breathalyzer and gave blood. I don't remember what his blood alcohol level was, but needless to say, it was two or three times the legal limit. He "slept it off," and by the time the Sergeant Major picked him up in jail, he was 100% sober and coherent.

That young man's military career ended that day. He was irresponsibly drinking alcohol and killed someone. Involuntary manslaughter. Had his idiot friend, who is a disgrace to the Special Operations community, taken Responsibility for his friend's irresponsibility… and stopped him from driving under the influence, that young lady would still be alive today. But ultimately, had Justin been more responsible with his alcohol consumption, he wouldn't have killed that innocent girl and ruined his life.

I can honestly report to you that I have never been drunk. So please don't associate heavy drinking with toughness or manliness. I love a nice glass of wine with dinner. But that's it … a glass. I simply don't understand why you would want to drink to the point that you lose control. Irresponsible drinking never ends well.

Quality Control

The afternoon shift in the quality control department at a prestigious automobile factory failed to identity that their welder robot was missing welding lines by three millimeters. Ten vehicle chassis were forwarded to the next department before the error was discovered. The production line manager called in two members of the quality control section, individually, to discuss the situation. One made an excuse, and the second took Responsibility. After completing the investigation, the robot was repaired and production resumed. The excuse-maker was allowed to keep his job, but was placed on six months of probation. The Responsibility-taker was promoted to team leader.

Husband & Father Responsibilities

In a story that we all know too well, a friend of mine, Jason, got his high school girlfriend pregnant. The baby was due a few months after high school graduation. When Jason told his parents the bad news and what they were thinking about doing, the parents panicked. The father slapped the son across the face and said he was ashamed of his irresponsibility. As the son laid on the ground, looking up at his father, the father made the plan.

Two weeks later, Jason and his girlfriend got married. They both graduated from high school, and when the baby was born, Jason was working forty hours a week at his new job and the couple was enjoying life in their new, cozy apartment. It was a difficult time in their lives, but they had each other and loving parents. Years later, they are still happily married, but with three beautiful kids. As you can imagine, Jason and his father are still very close. He looks back with shame that his father had to remind him of the rules of Responsibility, when he was trying to shirk it. He almost walked away from a wife and family, two sources of amazing joy. Thankfully, his father gave him a reminder that being a man requires taking Responsibility.

Jason initially wanted to shirk his Responsibility, but thankfully took it. Now let's move on to another family-based example of someone who starts out taking Responsibility and then later shirks it.

Edward, a business owner and former Marine, marries his university sweetheart and pledges to love and cherish her until death do they part. After twenty-five years of marriage and raising two boys, he decides he wants to upgrade his wife to a newer unit, someone younger. He finds a fun replacement, files for divorce, and kicks his wife out of the house.

In her sadness, the wife settles for a large sum of money that she doesn't take care of. Since the husband ran the money and finances for the past twenty-five years, she only worried about taking care of the household and being a good helpmate to her husband. She wasn't prepared for the sharks and pariahs who gave her bad financial advice and encouraged her to buy a new house way over market value. Within a year, she is back to work for the first time in twenty-five years. But since her education and experiences were twenty-five years out of date, she was only able to find a terrible job, one which she will have to suffer through until the day she dies, alone and brokenhearted.

Edward marries the woman with whom he had an affair. Of course, she didn't have a problem having sex with a married man, so why would she insist on getting a new "wedding bed" or furniture? Edward is lucky, he didn't even have to rearrange the furniture. He simply kicked out the old wife and moved in the new one.

As Edward's business keeps growing, the money flows in and his quality of life grows exponentially. Meanwhile, his ex-wife is financially and emotionally broken and alone. She will never love another. And she will work just to earn enough to survive until the day she dies. What a tragedy. And this happens every day, all over the world. Men are deliberately neglecting the Responsibility they vowed to their wives.

Individual Training / Development Plan: (PTREXAR)

Now is the point where you need to take a break from this book, sit down with a piece of paper, and make a plan on how you are going to train / develop the mindset of Responsibility. Use the below questions to help you make your plan.

If you are going to skip this section, then please at least answer the first question: Where am I the least responsible?

Plan:

- Where am I the least responsible?
- How can I be more responsible in that area?
- List three things I can do to be more responsible:
    - #1:
    - #2:
    - #3:
- How do I plan to accomplish each of the above?
    - Training Tasks / Behaviors / Actions?
    - Frequency of Training?
    - Milestones / Phases?
- How or where or in what situations can I rehearse showing or displaying Responsibility?
- What is the purpose of developing Responsibility?
- What is my ultimate Goal / End-State regarding Responsibility?
- How can I evaluate if my Responsibility training is working?

Train: Go out there and get to work. Start today. Do what you planned (above) to do. Train like you fight. Don't make this easy on yourself. Make your training harder and more difficult, so that when it becomes time to execute your goal, you will be overly prepared.

Rehearse: Put yourself in situations where you will be able to take Responsibility.

Execute: Execute that final display of Responsibility for which you have been planning. Accomplish your goal.

Analyze: Assess if your Responsibility has grown and developed. Analyze how effective your training plan was. What did you do wrong during this PTREXAR cycle? How can you improve next time?

Repeat: Now get out there and do the whole PTREXAR cycle again! Get even better!

9: Courage

During my third tour to Afghanistan, I had the honor of working in western Afghanistan with some of the most exceptional men I have ever met. During this deployment, I was the Executive Officer, the second in charge of a 500-man Special Operations Task Force comprised of Marine Raiders and Green Berets. Early into our six-month tour, a Marine Special Operations Team was badly ambushed by a large number of Taliban forces. We ordered a counterattack to the same objective the very next night. We could see from an unmanned arial vehicle (UAV) over the objective that the enemy forces spent the entire day digging in other IEDs, setting fighting positions, and preparing for a counterattack. It was going to be a huge fight.

The Army Special Forces team chosen to do the mission was one of the most aggressive and competent teams I ever worked with. Every member a seasoned combat vet, the team leader, team sergeant, and team warrant officer were second to none. As we discussed the mission, I never saw a glimpse of hesitation or fear. Only Competence and Courage. They spent the next twelve hours planning and rehearsing their mission.

After the sun set, they initiated movement to the objective with their Afghanistan Special Forces partners. Rather than driving into the city, where we knew the Taliban was waiting in various ambush positions, they stopped on the outskirts and attacked on foot. They went house by house, street by street, neighborhood by neighborhood, systematically and precisely destroying all enemy forces. Not one American Special Operator was hurt. No collateral damage.

Because SOF teams are small, they are usually used to conduct more surgical missions. But we had no choice to send them against a numerically superior threat. So, we made sure that they had a great plan, fire support, augmentation, heavy weapons, close air support, and UAV intelligence. I still think back to this mission and am thankful for answered prayers that no friendly forces were hurt or killed. I thought it was going to be a tragedy, one that people would write books about. Instead, it was such a success that no one has ever even heard of it. Had I not even mentioned it in these four short paragraphs, and believe me I grossly oversimplifying the importance and the top-secret aspects of this mission, it would have been another forgotten mission of courageous SOF quiet professionals doing what no one else in the world can do without even the slightest hint of fanfare or accolades.

Courageous men doing courageous missions is what SOF is all about.

Definition & Considerations

Courage can be defined as the "mental or moral strength to venture, persevere, and withstand danger, fear, or difficulty."[12] I am a fan of this definition because it touches on so many of the important nuances of Courage.

<u>Courage is conviction</u>. Webster calls it mental and moral strength. I like to call this conviction. Although Courage is a muscle that can be exercised and strengthened, it frequently manifests while being at the wrong place at the wrong time. Those anomalies where a normal man rushes into a burning building to save a child are not the result of rehearsal and training. They are actions that results from a mental or moral conviction. They value human life, and so they risk their own to save another's.

<u>Courage requires action</u>. Fighting the Taliban requires action. Jumping out of an airplane in the dark requires action. But so does standing up to a bully or overcoming social pressures. Saying, "No more, here I stand," takes action.

Courage frequently requires <u>endurance</u>. The Emancipation Proclamation was in 1862, yet we

---

[12] https://www.merriam-webster.com/dictionary/courage

are still having race riots over "Black Lives Matter" almost 160 years later. Fighting injustice and racism take perseverance.

East Germans were instantly separated from their friends and family when the Berlin Wall was built. It must have taken extreme Courage and persistence to wait out the years between 1961 and 1989.

<u>Courage is overcoming fear</u>. What I have learned over the years is that while fear may be subjective, it is real. What may be frightening to one person is not frightening to another. But to the frightened one, the fear is very real. For example, a fireman is trained to work in dangerous environments. He can see from the characteristics of a burning house that he has a certain amount of time to pull someone out. It still requires bravery to rescue someone from the building. But statistically, the building was not yet on the verge of collapse. Although he is still in a dangerous and volatile situation, his level of fear is relatively low.

<u>Courage through statistics</u>: I believe in statistics. You are more likely to survive a car accident if you wear your seatbelt and drive a big truck or SUV. You are more likely to survive a battle if you are wearing body armor and a helmet. You

are more likely to survive a bad parachute landing if you fly your parachute into the wind and wear a bump helmet. But how do these statistics relate to fear? We frequently are more courageous when we have statistics to back us up. Because I am not likely to die in a plane crash, I am more courageous when the plane hits heavy turbulence. Because I am not likely to die from a bad reaction to a vaccine, I am less afraid to get a shot. Statistics don't make you brave, but they may give you a bit more Courage than you would have had without them.

What it is

Courage is <u>doing the hard right over the easy wrong</u>. Everyone in class might be picking on or bullying the nerd. But the courageous person puts a stop to it. It might be easy to do certain things to fit in. But the courageous person does what is right, not what is popular or easy.

<u>Courage is action</u>. You can't just talk about Courage. It must be shown through action. These actions can be physical, as in pushing someone out of the way of an oncoming car. But they can also be ideological, as in publishing a document or book or video that speaks out against an injustice. Either way, Courage is only shown through what is done, said, produced, written, edited. Courage requires action.

Courage is taking Responsibility: Although I am a firm believer in choosing your battles, a person of Courage doesn't assume that someone else is going to solve the problem. They take Responsibility for the situation and do what is required to fix it.

What it isn't

Deferred Responsibility. Deferred Responsibility is when everyone assumes that someone else will take care of it. In the previous chapter we told the story of a woman being attacked and raped in an alley of a residential neighborhood in a large city. She screams for help. Several neighbors hear her yelling. They assume that someone else will call the police. But no one did. They deferred Responsibility to someone else. No one took action, and so the woman was badly assaulted.

Courage is not following the crowd. Most people would rather live in the valley. They want to be entertained, to fit in, to consume. They have no desire to put in the effort to rise to the occasion, to hike to the mountaintop and dwell on high. For this reason alone, courageous people don't follow the crowd. Every adult German you talk to admits that Hitler was evil. But how in the world did their grandparents follow his evil leadership?

They followed the crowd. And millions of innocents died.

Everyone loves cheap products from China. But who has the Courage to confront their continuous human right violations?

Best Indicators Of

The best indicator of Courage is <u>Confidence</u>. If you are confident that you are right, then you have will have the Courage to speak out. If you are confident in your abilities to win on the battlefield, then you will have the Courage to leave the firebase.

Another indicator of Courage is <u>confrontation</u>. Courageous people will make others mad. Because they don't follow the crowd, they will eventually ruffle feathers and offend. If you get along with everyone, then likely you don't have any Courage and don't stand firm for anything. You are a yes man, an appeaser. As I stated a few paragraphs earlier, I think it is wise to pick your battles. But for sure, a courageous person is going to have battles.

Too Much or Too Little

<u>Too much Courage, and you are a fool</u>. This is true on so many levels. The young are often foolish with the way they think. They haven't seen their friends die. They have never been in a major car accident. So, they aren't afraid to drive and text at the same time. They aren't afraid to drive in the snow in the same manner they would drive on a sunny day. We also see overly courageous people die every year rock climbing. They are too confident in their abilities and slip off the rock to their death. Had they not been overly confident, they would have taken appropriate safety precautions and still be alive today.

<u>Too little Courage, and you are a coward</u>. Perhaps you have heard the proverb "If you don't stand for something, you will fall for anything." A person without Courage or conviction or belief will never be able to take a leap of faith or do the hard right over the easy wrong.

Implications Of

If you are courageous, then you are going to (1) accomplish more, (2) have conflict, and (3) go where others don't have the Courage to go.

<u>Accomplish More</u>: You can't succeed if you don't try. Only those who have the Courage to

attempt something will ever have the possibility of accomplishing it. If you have the Courage to try something, then you are so much more likely to succeed. You may fail a time or two. But eventually you will reach your goal.

Conflict: A person of Courage acts in accordance with conviction. This will cause them to stand out from the crowd. And standing out from the crowd will inevitably cause conflict. Someone with the Courage to live a life of integrity will get ridiculed by those who like to cheat on their taxes. Those with the Courage to speak out against human rights violations will always fight with those who violate human rights. If you have Courage, you will put it to use. If you don't have Courage, you will live a peaceful life with the rest of the sheep. That is, until slaughter time.

Go Where Others Don't Have the Courage to Go: Because a person of Courage attempts more and accomplishes more, they will go where others only dream of going and do that which others only dream of doing. Imagine a small-town family. One child has the Courage to leave and explore the world. One resents her life because she never left.

How It's Built

<u>Courage is built by making a Commitment</u>. This Commitment is often religious, philosophical, or practical. As we learned earlier, a Commitment is making a promise and "following through" with it. A Commitment is making a pledge to do something and "following through" with it. A Commitment is making a firm decision to do something and then "following through" with it. A Commitment is acknowledging your moral obligation to do something and then "following through" with it. This "follow-through" is where you will most frequently be able to show and build Courage. If you make a Commitment to your family, for sure you will be attacked by those who want to steal from them, exploit them, hurt them. It will take Courage to fight back. If you make a Commitment to human rights, then for sure you will see injustices and feel obligated to say or do something to stop it.

<u>Courage is built through integrity</u>. If you are undivided and have strong moral principles, then you will have to live (follow through) in accordance with your beliefs. And this will, for sure, require Courage. This is a person doing the hard right over the easy wrong. This is a person challenging the status quo. This is a person who refuses to accept governments and powerbrokers taking away someone's freedom or human rights.

Courage is built by doing hard things. The first time you stand up to a bully, an alcoholic father, or an abusive husband, it is going to be frightening. But the tenth time you do it, it will be much easier. Perhaps you train and develop the fighting skills to give the bully a beatdown. Perhaps you find the Courage to leave your alcoholic father or report your abusive husband to the police. The Confidence and Competence you get from doing hard things will always better prepare you for dangerous or frightening situations. The harder you train in peace, the better prepared you will be for war.

Infiltration Methods

A Marine has the Courage to parachute out of an airplane into the pitch-black night with a fifty-pound rucksack and a seven-pound rifle because he trusts the Rigger who prepared his parachute, the Pilots who fly his airplane, and the Jumpmaster who identified the Drop Zone (DZ). He jumps because he is committed to the mission and to the brothers on his team who jump before and after him.

An Airforce Pararescueman has the Courage to slide down the fast rope onto a steep mountain covered in snow and rush into an existing firefight to rescue a downed pilot because he has overcome his fear through hard training and is committed to doing his duty to protect his comrades in arms.

The Entrepreneur

A young man sees an opportunity to make a successful business. But he is still eighteen months away from graduating from his prestigious college. His parents will be so mad at him if he doesn't at least graduate first. But if he waits one more year, then someone else might go live with his idea. He finally decides to drop out of school to focus on his business idea. It takes a lot of Courage to drop out of school to focus on his business idea. But it pays off. A year later, he is a billionaire.

It takes a lot of Courage to start a new business. But if you are convinced of your business idea and put your Commitment into action, then you will have the Courage to quit school or your day job and pursue your entrepreneurial endeavor.

As discussed earlier, too much Courage is foolishness. So please only start a business and "go for it" if you have done your research to see if your business idea is viable. But if it is, then take that first step of faith and go for it.

Faithful Parents

Having integrity as a family is so difficult these days. It takes a lot of Courage to constantly fight away bad ideas and philosophies. Imagine a Christian couple trying to raise children in modern times. The world teaches so many values that fight against what they believe. For example, the world says that getting likes and followers on social media is the approval that matters. But the Christian parents teach their children that God's approval is what matters. The world says that you should do whatever you want to be happy. The Christian parents teach their children that living in accordance with biblical principles is the best way to be truly happy. The world says to use people and love material things. The Christian parents teach their kids to use things and love people. The world says to sleep around and keep your options open. The Christian parents teach loyalty and Commitment. It takes a lot of Courage to stand out from the crowd.

Individual Training / Development Plan: (PTREXAR)

Now is the point where you need to take a break from this book, sit down with a piece of paper, and make a plan on how you are going to train / develop the mindset of Courage. Use the below questions to help you make your plan.

If you are going to skip this section, then please at least answer the first question: Where am I the least courageous?

<u>Plan</u>:
- Where am I the least courageous?
- How can I improve my Courage in that area?
- List three things I can do to increase my Courage:
    - # 1:
    - # 2:
    - # 3:
- How do I plan to accomplish each of the above?
    - Training Tasks / Behaviors / Actions?
    - Frequency of Training?
    - Milestones / Phases?
- How or where or in what situations can I rehearse showing or displaying Courage?
- What is the purpose of developing Courage?
- What is my ultimate Goal / End-State regarding Courage?
- How can I evaluate if my Courage training is working?

Train: Go out there and get to work. Start today. Do what you planned (above) to do? Train like you fight. Don't make this easy on yourself. Make your training harder and more difficult, so that when it becomes time to execute your goal, you will be overly prepared.

Rehearse: Put yourself in situations where you will be able to demonstrate Courage.

Execute: Execute that final display of Courage for which you have been planning. Accomplish your goal.

Analyze: Assess if your Courage has grown and developed. Analyze how effective your training plan was. What did you do wrong during this PTREXAR cycle? How can you improve next time?

Repeat: Now get out there and do the whole PTREXAR cycle again! Get even better!

10: Intensity

We were a few weeks into the Combat Diver Qualification Course (CDQC) at the Special Forces Underwater Operations Training Facility in Key West, Florida when I learned an insightful lesson about Intensity from the cashier at the dining facility. At that time, when we would rush through the dining facility for our meals, we would tell that cashier the last four numbers of our Social Security number and what military branch we were in. I wasn't exactly sure why, but I think this was so that the Army dining facility, on a Navy installation, could properly bill Air Force and Army students differently for their meals.

I was in a joking mood when it was my turn and said, "3489 Air Force."

Without hesitation, the fifty-year-old Hispanic lady working the cashier replied, "No you're not. You're Army."

I was surprised that she so quickly knew that I was Army, not Air Force. So, I asked her if she remembered me from before. She said that she didn't remember me, and that it is easy to tell who was Air Force and who was Army.

So, I challenged her. Pointing to the next few guys in line, who were all wearing the same terrible dive shorts and a brown issued t-shirt, I asked her to say if they were Army or Air Force.

She confidently began "Army. Army. Army. Air Force. Air Force. Army. Definitely Air Force, Definitely Air Force. Air Force. Army. Definitely Army."

She was 100% correct, despite us all being in the same uniform. I was very impressed but gave her a curious look.

She leaned in closer to me and told me her secret. "Yes, you guys are all in great shape and in the same uniform, but the Air Force guys are doing this SCUBA school at the beginning of their training pipeline. The Army guys are doing this school at the end of their training or after years on a team. The Air Force guys are all scared. They're timid. Some try to hide it, but you can easily see it in their eyes. But you Army guys are intense, too intense. Confident. Not afraid at all. For the most part, you all look like you are ready for any challenge in the world."

I was impressed. What she said was very true. All jokes aside referencing the Air Force, the fact is that we are all more confident at the end of our training than at the beginning. Half the Army guys in my dive class were combat vets, and the other half were guys like me, who had been treated so badly in the past year of constant training that no matter what they did to us, we couldn't be scared or broken.

Definition & Considerations

Intensity is defined as "the quality of being <u>extreme in strength or force</u>" or "the quality of being very serious and <u>having strong emotions or opinions</u>."[13] These are also great words we could use to describe Special Operators: "extreme in strength or force," "serious … having strong emotions or opinions."

When you see SOF in action, there is no doubt regarding their <u>extreme strength or force</u>. They don't ask permission for a bomb maker to surrender. They kick in his door, bum-rush him in the middle of the night, zip-tie his hands and feet, put a bag over his head to prevent him from seeing anything or anyone, and throw him in a helicopter to go get his due justice. And anyone who gets in their way receives the same treatment or worse. You can't be the best of the best without a prerequisite of strength and force.

---

[13] https://dictionary.cambridge.org/dictionary/english/Intensity

<u>Intensity requires passion</u>. There is no such thing as "Yeah, okay, whatever." Lackadaisical attitudes are fine for deciding if you are going to go to your favorite Mexican restaurant or to a steak house. But when it comes to important matters, there is "HELL YES, LET'S DO IT!" That is the response of an intense person.

What it is

<u>Intensity is internal</u>. No one can give it to you. Of course, you can be inspired. But inspiration wears off; Intensity doesn't. It comes from deep within and is fueled by your individual purpose and Motivation.

Intensity also <u>requires focus</u>. Staying focused on the tasks at hand while freeing yourself from distraction is a requirement for mission accomplishment. Easily distracted people never become Elite Performers. They spend most of their free time in front of the television being distracted or entertained. Lazy people never become SOF because they can never stay focused on their mission.

Intensity <u>is competitive</u>. Some who are intense like to challenge others. They join teams and have extreme hobbies. But the ultra-intense are only competitive with themselves. They push themselves in everything they do. They are competing against themselves in their never-ending quest for excellence.

Intensity is <u>driven</u>. It is driven by that personal Motivation or purpose that helps the bearer focus on the goal, eliminate distraction, and accomplish the mission. When doing extreme or great deeds, it is always important to know your purpose. Knowing why you are doing something will always help you drive on in the hard times.

Intensity is <u>being in the moment</u>. When you can ignore the peripheral and focus on the present, you will be much more alert and participative. It is fun to see the difference between talking to a normal person and talking with a member of Special Operations. Their face is intense. They are leaning forward. They are actively listening, often with a skeptical or serious look on their face. They make the kind of eye contact that encourages people to step back. They are in the moment. And although it might not be as interesting to them as jumping out of a plane or shooting guns from a moving vehicle, they are intense people and it even shows in their conversations.

Intensity is <u>active</u>. You simply can't be intense about something and then sit on your sofa and watch more television. If you truly are intense about a matter, then you turn your passion into action. You fight for civil liberties. You free the oppressed. You finish that next school course. You train for that next deployment. Intensity without action isn't Intensity. It's just talk.

What it isn't

<u>Intensity isn't talk</u>. It isn't saying something loudly or with a lot of bad words.

Intensity <u>is not easily distracted</u>. When you are focused, energized, and passionate about something, you make it happen. You aren't distracted by the typical things that consume the time and lives of normal people. A passionate writer stays up all night finishing a new chapter. A passionate athlete trains harder than his colleagues who are in it for the money. An intense soldier never stops improving his situation or working for the good of his team. They aren't distracted away from doing what they so intensely want or need to do.

<u>Intensity can't be faked</u>. Either you are passionate about something and will keep at it, or you are lying to yourself and will quit when the going gets tough.

Best Indicators Of

The best indicator of Intensity is <u>action</u>. You keep going in good times and in bad times. You don't quit. Every day is progress. Every situation is a training opportunity. Your actions are the best way to see that you are driven to do and to accomplish.

Another indicator of Intensity is <u>purpose</u>. If you are intense, then you don't fiddle around with finding a purpose. You know your purpose. You don't have to seek false Motivation because you are internally motivated.

Intense people have a never-ending source of <u>energy</u>. They work harder and longer than their counterparts. They don't quit or go home when the whistle blows and their shift is over. They keep going until they are satisfied.

Too Much or Too Little

Too much Intensity and you are obsessive. If everything is 100%, every decision 100%, every situation 100%, then the people around you are going to resent your presence. There needs to be some balance. Most SOF guys I know are easygoing and humble about unimportant and routine decisions of life. But for the decisions and situations that really matter, they are 100%, black and white.

Too little Intensity and you are docile. This is the passive father who has relegated leading the family to the wife. This is the twenty-year-old boy who still doesn't have his driver's license and who spends all of his spare time playing video games. This is the millions of people who watch life go by on their television rather than experiencing it for themselves.

Implications Of

If you are intense, then you are going to (1) waste less time, and (2) accomplish more.

<u>Waste less time</u>: If you are intense, then you want and need to get "it" done. The "it" is different for everyone, but for sure it is not watching television and sleeping in until noon. The flock is reactive and goes where it is led. The intense person makes his own path. He doesn't wait for others to tell him what to do.

<u>Accomplish more</u>: Someone who is driven to be the best will always accomplish more than someone who isn't. They will work harder, train harder, learn more. They will push themselves to do and to make. Because they are motivated and know their purpose, they will become more competent and more efficient. And this, too, will ensure that they accomplish more than their less intense colleagues or peers.

How It's Built

<u>Intensity is built through actions</u>, not words. Something needs to be done. You don't talk about it; you just do it. Then something else needs to be done. You don't procrastinate, you just do it. As this becomes a pattern in your life, you soon see that actions are significantly more effective than words or procrastination. You will become a doer, not a watcher. And this is the first step in becoming an intense person.

<u>Intensity is built by knowing your purpose</u>. Self-driven people know why they are working so hard and are so focused on accomplishing. If you are looking for Motivation to do something, then you need to start with understanding your purpose for doing and or your purpose for being.

Intensity is <u>built through competition</u>. But the best kind of competition is with yourself: a deep longing to be better. If you are constantly and continuously raising and challenging your personal standards, you will develop an inner drive to be the best.

Switched On

I first learned about being "switched on" during the Special Forces Advanced Urban Combat Course. The head instructor told us: "Before you blow a charge and go through the door, you better be switched on. Relax and do a good job of planning and preparation. But when it is go-time, flip that Intensity switch in your brain and focus on the mission."

What he was talking about is that while most of the time a Special Operator is intense, there are times where your focus and attention to detail and flow need to be switched on. Your strength and force need to be dialed all the way to 100%.

Being "switched on" is not just applicable to a team of Green Berets kicking in the door of a known terrorist arms dealer. It can also apply to a father protecting his family, a student defending his doctorate, a manager giving his sales pitch. There simply are times where the stakes are higher and the Intensity and focus supercharger needs to be switched on.

The Perfectionist

One of my best friends from high school, James, owns a very successful and well-respected luxury home construction company which bears his name, James York Construction. He says that he named the company after himself so that if anyone has a customer service complaint or a quality control issue, they will know who to blame.

A gentleman by nature, James is intense and demanding. He never settles, and only the best work and best materials are accepted for his builds. Although the construction community is full of some rough and tough types, James never shies away from a confrontation:

"I don't care if it passed code. Code is the minimum standard. And around here, we both know it is a joke. We build the best and only perfection will do. So, redo your sloppy work or I will. If you redo it, I will appreciate your Commitment to nothing but the best. But if I redo your work, we'll never subcontract to you ever again."

"The choice is yours. But it is my name on the sign out there and I'm not accepting anything less than perfection."

Well done, James. I wish everyone would so intensely protect their reputation and the integrity of their work.

The Obsessed Ice Skater

When I was at Harvard, the school of government rented an entire outdoor skating rink for two hours one Saturday morning. It was a social event to bring students together. Skates were free. All you had to do was show up. Being from Arizona,

I was never really exposed to or good at ice-skating. But I thought this might be a fun opportunity to get better.

Of course, I showed up punctually at 10 a.m. The problem was that it was freezing outside, -2 degrees Fahrenheit (-18C). I was the only one who showed up. "Great," I thought. "More space for me."

I tried on my skates and went out for some laps. After a few minutes, I was having fun and doing pretty well. Then I started getting into the zone [the "Intensity" zone]. I started doing drills. It started with going clockwise and making big strides left over right. Then I went counterclockwise, making big strides right over left. Then I started to work on my starts and stops. Then sprinting. After about an hour of drills, one other student showed up with his girlfriend. Thankfully he was a friend of mine.

"Christopher? What is going on? You are soaking wet?

In my ill-fated desire to become a world-class hockey player after an hour of drills, I sweated through all of my clothes.

I excused myself from the rink, slipped on my boots, and returned to my apartment to shower and "freshen up."

The point of this story is that sometimes I get "switched on" and too focused on my training. I am intense and I like to get better at the things I do. I run training drills for everything I do, even ice skating. If you are the type of guy who is happy to show up at a skating rink and do a couple of laps, then Special Operations and Elite Performance is not for you. But if you find yourself doing drills and pushing yourself in everything you do, then you might have found your tribe.

Individual Training / Development Plan: (PTREXAR)

Now is the point where you need to take a break from this book, sit down with a piece of paper, and make a plan on how you are going to train / develop the mindset of Intensity. If you think it is awkward to plan for Intensity, then consider its opposite … passivity. Instead of working on Intensity, consider where you are passive and want to be more active. Use the below questions to help you make your plan.

If you are going to skip this section, then please at least answer the first question: Where am I the least intense?

Plan:
- Where am I the least intense (... or most passive / reactive)?
- How can I improve my Intensity in that area?
- List three things I can do to increase my Intensity (or not be passive / reactive):
    - #1:
    - #2:
    - #3:
- How do I plan to accomplish each of the above?
    - Training Tasks / Behaviors / Actions?
    - Frequency of Training?
    - Milestones / Phases?
- How or where or in what situations can I rehearse showing or displaying Intensity (or not being passive / reactive)?
- What is the purpose of developing Intensity (or not being passive / reactive)?
- What is my ultimate Goal / End-State regarding Intensity?
- How can I evaluate if my Intensity training is working?

Train: Go out there and get to work. Start today. Do what you planned (above) to do. Train like you fight. Don't make this easy on yourself. Make your training harder and more difficult, so that when it becomes time to execute your goal, you will be overly prepared.

Rehearse: Put yourself in situations where you will be able to demonstrate Intensity.

Execute: Execute that final display of Intensity for which you have been planning. Accomplish your goal.

Analyze: Assess if your Intensity has grown and developed. Analyze how effective your training plan was. What did you do wrong during this PTREXAR cycle? How can you improve next time?

Repeat: Now get out there and do the whole PTREXAR cycle again! Get even better!

11: Mental Toughness

I went through the Special Forces Combat Diver Qualification Course (CDQC) with a man who embodied Mental Toughness, let's call him Scott. Scott had been on a SCUBA team for six months before going to dive school. Scott loved his new team and would do anything to honor them and to be able to remain on the team. Obviously, it was important to Scott to finish training.

Scott was so committed to graduating from CDQC that he basically said to himself, "I'm leaving here with my SCUBA bubble or I'm leaving here in body bag." This is a great example of Commitment.

Scott was not the best swimmer or diver by a long shot. Skills that came easily to some were exceptionally difficult to him. Yet, Scott had more Commitment than anyone else in the course. I personally saw him pass out under water three times. Each time, he was pulled out of the pool, revived with a little oxygen, and sent back in a few minutes later for retraining. What Courage he displayed getting back into the pool a few minutes later. His Courage was inspiring.

What took his Mental Toughness to the next level was the fact that Scott's father died in a SCUBA diving accident while on vacation, when Scott was fifteen years old. Wow. Every time Scott got back into the water, he must have thought about how his father died. And yet, he was mentally tough enough to keep going, to drive on. Scott was one of the mentally toughest men I have ever met.

Definition & Considerations

Toughness is defined as "the physical or emotional strength that allows someone to endure strain or hardship," and "the quality of being strong and not easily broken."[14] I like that Webster's dictionary focuses on both enduring strain and not being easily broken.

<u>Enduring Strain</u>: It is impossible to develop Mental Toughness without hardship. If you have never had to deal with adversity, you are going to be a weak sister. Better to have endured challenges than to have had a soft and cushy life where everything is fed to you with a golden spoon. One of the reasons many young kids these days are so mentally weak is because their loving parents have pampered them into feebleness.

---

[14] https://www.merriam-webster.com/dictionary/toughness

Not Easily Broken: Someone who is mentally tough is not easily broken. You can yell at him (as in basic training), yet he will keep driving on. You can make him do impossible physical deeds (as in Special Operations training) and he will accomplish them. You can take away everything he owns and all his material possessions (as in living out of a rucksack for a six-month deployment) and he will never complain. You can make him push his body and mind to the absolute limit (as in leadership in a war zone) and he will continue to perform marvelously. And this unbreakable spirit is why Special Operators can do anything.

Mental toughness requires Truth: We discussed in chapter 2: "Truth" the importance of not lying to yourself. It is impossible to become mentally tough if you lie to yourself. Yes, I am getting fat. I need to get into amazing shape. No, I am not a good swimmer. I need to work on my endurance in the pool. I'm totally scared to jump out of plane and would never do that. I don't want a conflict with my stepmother, so I will just stay away from my dad. I'm not getting promoted at work because I don't care about it. I need to take more ownership and Responsibility.

Confidence: Mental Toughness is closely related to Confidence. You build Mental Toughness alongside Confidence as you do hard things. The nuance is that to build Mental Toughness, these "hard things" must be physically and mentally demanding. For example, you can build Confidence by setting a hard goal and accomplishing it, as in graduating from a university. But this doesn't make you mentally tough. Mental Toughness comes from enduring a hardship, as well as by accomplishing hard tasks and surviving adversity.

<u>Mental Toughness often requires confrontation</u>. Many people these days hate confrontation and avoid it at all costs. They keep their mouths shut for the sake of peace and end up getting stepped on or disrespected. They would rather capitulate than argue. Mental Toughness comes from overcoming or enduring a confrontation. Imagine a Drill Sergeant who says you are a loser and will never finish basic training. He clearly hates you and wants to make your life miserable. Imagine a work colleague who makes a flippant political statement that violates everything you stand for. Walking away makes you an assertive person, and for sure there is a time and place to be assertive. But if you stick up for your yourself and for your beliefs, then you are going to be mentally tougher.

"<u>If you are going to be stupid, you better be tough</u>." This is one of my favorite mottos. I like to repeat it to myself whenever I crash my mountain bike, tumble down the mountain on my snowboard, or when my back and shoulders ache after a long ruck-march. Enduring the pain of life is also a way to get mentally tougher. I guarantee that a Marine Raider complains less after an emergency appendectomy than the average person.

<u>The inside cat -vs- the outside cat</u>. A house cat will suffer when the veterinarian gives them their annual shot. An outside cat won't even blink. This is because the inside cat only knows a warm and safe house, food from a bag or can, and sleeps on a soft couch or pad every day. The outside cat sleeps and lives in the heat, the rain, the snow. He climbs trees with splinters and walks by plants with thorns. He's toughened himself to the point that a vaccine needle is nothing more than the same nonexistent sting he gets from walking through sharp leaves as he goes to his favorite hunting ground.

I see this phenomenon a lot in the military. Two buddies graduate from the conventional Army medic course and are stationed at Fort Bragg. One medic gets assigned to the hospital. He works eight-hour shifts, five days a week. He calls his team leader, a Staff Sergeant, and his Doctor, a Major, by their first name. He does PT on his own. His buddy, on the other hand, gets assigned to an Infantry Battalion in the 82nd Airborne Division. He does ninety minutes of crushing PT every day, works twelve to sixteen hours every day, gets treated like an infantryman but with the extra benefit of carrying a twenty-five-pound medic's bag on top of his rucksack. He goes to Airborne school and Ranger school. He gets deployed for eighteen months, where he lives out of his rucksack for weeks on end. And because he is a medic, he is sent on every mission.

The hospital medic, in this case, becomes an inside cat. He has rights and privileges and is a weakling. He might get promoted, but he will never accomplish anything great. The Airborne Ranger medic is the outside cat. He has learned to deal with terrible and heavy situations, and for the rest of his life he is mentally tough enough to accomplish anything to which he sets his mind.

<u>Resilience</u>: Resilience is a trendy word these days, gaining popularity in politically correct circles, to include the U.S. government and military. Resilience is defined as "the capability of a strained body to recover its size and shape after deformation caused especially by compressive stress." Think of a rubber damper in a shock absorber system that's smashed over and over again, yet if it is resilient enough, it will bounce back into form. When applying this concept to

human psychology, we define it as the "ability to recover from or adjust easily to misfortune or change."[15] Think of a Marine who is saddened because his battle buddy is killed, yet he bounces back and is able to perform throughout the rest of the deployment.

Intelligent people and the mentally tough are resilient. Dumb people are never resilient. People who are not able to put a situation, event, or tragedy into perspective are never resilient. People who are mentally weak are never resilient. But if you are mentally tough, you are resilient.

I want to quickly clarify something. Tragedies are real. There are hundreds of things worse than death. I'm not trying to belittle these tragedies. What I am trying to say is that someone who is mentally tough is able to get keep going. At "Life is a Special Operation," we believe that life is special. Life is a gift from God. Even during and after challenges and obstacles, life is always worth living. This is why we see mentally tough soldiers recover from tragedies and explosions on the battlefield and go on to live happy and productive lives. This is why we see mentally tough wives continue on after the death of their husbands. This is why we see mentally tough

---

[15] https://www.merriam-webster.com/dictionary/resilience

trainees bounce back after a failed training evolution and go on to pass the next.

Comfort Zone: The tendency of most people is to stay in their comfort zone. They don't try harder things or undertake great feats because they are happy to stay comfortable. When you step outside your comfort zone, regardless of whether or not you succeed or fail, your comfort zone will grow larger. And as your comfort zone grows, so will your Confidence and peace grow in uncomfortable situations.

Basic Training / Boot Camp: A classic example for building Mental Toughness is Basic Training. Even if you have never been to Basic Training, we all remember stereotypical movies scenes where a hardened Drill Sergeant yells at a scared and fragile recruit. After weeks of enduring mental harassment, the recruit gains a newfound toughness. It is a bit cliché, but there is still Truth in the methodology. Endure mental harassment, and you will be mentally tough. This is one reason why kids these days are so mentally weak and fragile. Their helicopter parents protect them from the world so much so that they never have to endure an argument, a fight, or worse yet, learning the Truth that they aren't the best and brightest at everything in the world. I'm not prescribing boot camp or Basic Training for everyone. The Truth is, Basic Training is a joke when compared with Special Operations training. But to those who have never had to endure hardship or opposition, it is a big deal to stand at attention while someone yells at you.

What it is

Mental Toughness is being able to endure hardship.

Mental Toughness is bouncing back into shape after getting smashed. Recover. Learn from what just happened. Hold your head up high. And drive on.

Mental Toughness is being strong enough to handle the Truth. It might not be what you want to hear, but it corresponds to reality and is a good starting point. You can't be the best at everything. But for sure, you should never settle for lies about your Competence and skills.

Mental Toughness is not backing down when you know you are right.

Mental Toughness is doing something difficult and new, already knowing that you can accomplish it. This comes from having already tried and accomplished other difficult challenges in the past.

Mental Toughness is being comfortable with the uncomfortable. This is mental comfort, best trained through enduring physical discomfort.

Mental Toughness is being confident in new and uncomfortable situations. But remember, Confidence must be real, and based upon capabilities and skills.

Mental Toughness is having Courage to act in ambiguous, dangerous, or uncomfortable situations.

Mental Toughness is when you woman-up or man-up!

What it isn't

Mental Toughness is not being broken just because you had a failure or setback or negative feedback.

Mental Toughness is not being a jerk. Just because you are harder and tougher and more resilient than others, doesn't give you the right to be a jerk about it.

Mental Toughness isn't talking trash. A lot of people try to pretend to be tough, mentally and physically. But they aren't. They talk tough, but aren't. The toughest people I know don't talk about how tough they are. They show it through their actions.

Best Indicators Of

<u>The best indicator of Mental Toughness is Confidence.</u> After you have done hard things, after you have fallen off the horse and gotten back up again, after you have overcome difficult challenges, schools, training, events and or tragedies, you learn that you can withstand, endure, or do so much more than you thought possible. And this builds Confidence.

Another indicator of Mental Toughness is <u>resilience</u>. When you are crushed, you bounce back into shape. When you fall off the horse, you get back on. When you endure a tragedy, you see the bigger picture and keep driving on.

A final indicator of Mental Toughness is <u>peace</u>. If you are confident in your abilities and mental strength, then you are going to have peace in uncomfortable situations and in the face of future adversities.

Too Much or Too Little

Too little Mental Toughness and you are a wimp, a pushover. We see this in people who have no opinions, people who follow the crowd and never stand up for what they know is right.

Too much Mental Toughness and you become insensitive, always getting annoyed at how weak most people are. To a man who has hiked Mount Everest, people are weak if they complain about being tired after a long day of shopping. To a Navy Seal, people are being silly if they wear a dry suit to SCUBA dive in warm Caribbean water. To a woman who has endured hardship and worked incredibly hard to build her business, most entrepreneurs are quitters who lack Commitment and Discipline.

Implications Of

If you are mentally tough, then you are going to (1) accomplish more, (2) be confident, (3) and be resilient.

Accomplish More: People who quit at the first sight of adversity or challenge never succeed at anything. If you are able to deal with adversity, you will push through it to success. If you are able to endure hard challenges and events, then you will overcome them and accomplish your goal.

Be Confident: Endurance produces Confidence. If you overcome adversity and challenges, then you automatically are a stronger and more confident person, better able to repeat the same process. As we mentioned in the chapter on Confidence, doing hard things is the best way to build Confidence. Similarly, enduring hard things also produces Confidence because you learned that you are able to overcome and that you are stronger than you thought.

<u>Be Resilient</u>: Everyone fails. But the weak person fails and decides to never try again. The strong person gets back up and goes after it. A cowboy gets back on the horse after he has been bucked off. A mentally tough person knows his worth. He picks himself up after a fall and keeps going.

How It's Built

Mental Toughness is built by doing hard things … repeatedly. This is a vague answer, but it is true. Perhaps it is going through Special Operations training. Perhaps it is standing up to a bully. Perhaps it is moving out. Perhaps it is rigorous physical fitness or a marathon or an ultramarathon.

Mental Toughness is built through confrontation. Your teacher says you will never amount to anything, like your dad. But you rise above and graduate with honors. The Drill Sergeant says you are an idiot and a loser. But you rise above and finish Basic Training. The cadre at Ranger school treat you like trash and reminds you frequently that you are not tough enough to be a Ranger. But you Ranger-up! The first time you stick up for someone or confront a bully, you might be afraid of the consequences. But after you do it enough times, it becomes second nature.

Mental Toughness is built by facing your fears. If something scares you, then confront it. Don't shy away and be a wimp. Man-up! Woman-up! Confront your fear. Even if you get the beatdown, you will learn from it and be tougher for it. But with enough training and preparation, you just might overcome your fear and take your Mental Toughness to the next level.

Mental Toughness is built through suffering. This is why most young people are so mentally weak. This is why there are so many psychologists and employees with "burnout syndrome." The perfect breeding ground for mentally weak humans is a politically correct culture with a high standard of living, where your life is all about positive reinforcement (social media), your friends confirm and reconfirm every bad decision you make, you've never been hungry, you've never slept in a cold, wet or dangerous place, you avoid conflict and argument, and you have never been in a fight. This is why the poor are mentally tougher than the affluent. They have to work for what they want and need. Most of the men strong enough to make it through Special Operations training are from middle-class or poorer families. They weren't born with a silver spoon in their mouths. They knew hardship before they even joined the military. They had to learn Mental Toughness as a kid, and they keep developing it to the point that they can endure the hardest training in the world.

Mental Toughness is realizing that you are stronger than you thought. By confronting your fears, overcoming challenges, and enduring suffering, you realize that you are stronger and tougher than you thought.

Mental Toughness is built by going without. When you go on a three-to-ten-month deployment, you often only get to bring a few bags of gear with you. You keep a "B-Bag" or foot locker back at the base, and you take what you need for your mission in your rucksack or backpack. After a while, that is your world. You don't need anything else. Going without makes you tough and helps you to put life into perspective. And then when you return home, you realize how rich you are. Rather than sleeping on the ground or on a cot, you have a bed. Rather than wearing the same uniform for a week, you have fresh clothes.

You can eat what you want, go where you want, do what you want.

A good friend of mine, also a Special Forces Officer, loves his family and has tried his best to always provide them. But a few years ago, while stationed at the Pentagon, he thought that his kids were not appreciative of all that he and his wife provided for them. So, he set up the family tent in the backyard of their house in D.C. and the entire family moved in for a week. He called it "house appreciation training." Cooking on a camp stove. Sleeping and doing homework in the same space. No showers. They even had three days of rainstorms. The shock therapy worked. All the kids learned to appreciate their lives. It is no surprise that the daughter and oldest son went to West Point and are now Officers, and the younger son has turned into an amazing young man.

I feel obligated at this point to give a warning. Doing hard things doesn't mean doing stupid things. So be safe. Plan ahead. Mitigate risk. Prepare and train for it. Then get out there and do some hard stuff. Build some toughness, mental and physical.

Rangers Lead the Way

I'll never forget finishing Ranger school. I was lean, aggressive. I didn't need sleep. Ranger school taught me that sleep wasn't as much of a priority as I thought it was. I didn't need food. Ranger school taught me that food was a luxury that I could live without for much longer than just a few hours. I didn't need a nice or warm or dry or safe place to sleep. I was a warrior and I brought safety with me.

Decades later, I still think back to Ranger school and what I learned there. Yes, I love to eat good food. I even have a pillowtop bed. Luxury is nice. I enjoy it. But I know that I don't need it. And if / when the times require it … I'll give it all up and get back to work.

Resilience Incarnate

I want to give another illustration of Mental Toughness by telling a quick story about one of the men I went through the Special Forces Courses with, a dear friend, a true warrior. Let's call him Captain David. Born into a farming family in Nebraska, at six feet, 220 pounds, David was the smallest person in his family. He enlisted right out of high school, finished his university degree in his spare time, and was the only Officer Candidate School (OCS) student who had a

Combat Infantryman's Badge from his tour during the first Gulf War. Although he was a very kind-hearted man, he was a warrior. And as long as you didn't flip his Intensity switch, you never had anything to worry about. But when he was "switched on," you better get out of the way.

David was and is one of the most mentally tough men on earth. I saw this toughness in combative training, in the Special Forces Qualification Course, and repeatedly during his eight combat tours. But I really got to see how exceptional David was while observing him at the "finish line" of an extraordinary training event. Out of respect for the secretive nature of one of the training events, I do not want to disclose what course it is or to give too much context for this illustration. Let me just say that having been a prior participant, I was able to be at the finish line for several of my friends when they crossed the finish line.

Normally, at the finish line, the students are exhausted, worn down, beat down. It takes about five minutes for any Special Operators to realize his success and to relax, take a deep breath, and hold his head up high. If I've seen it once, I've seen it a hundred times. The transition from exhausted student to victorious graduate takes everyone a few minutes. But not so with David.

David crossed the finish line and walked straight over to a barrel full of ice water. He ripped off his nasty shirt, throwing it on the ground, splashed some cold water on his face, ran his fingers through his hair, stood up straight, took a deep breath, bowed back his shoulders, looked around, and was back. David took the physical and psychological journey in five seconds that the toughest and best warriors of the Special Operations community usually take in five minutes. There was not even a hint of fear or hesitation or exhaustion in his eyes. Just the fire of a genuine Confidence that can't and will never be extinguished.

Sure, challenges will come and go. But the toughest man I ever met will always have his head up and shoulders back as he moves out to attack the day and enjoy his life.

The Business App

Luke, an Information Technology (IT) programmer at a Fortune 500 company, does the honorable thing and gives his two-weeks' notice. He has been miserable during the past year because every time he brings up a good idea to his boss, his boss shuts him down, or berates him and then shuts him down. He knows he can make the project better, but the boss is a tyrant who enjoys belittling his staff.

The boss accepts Luke's resignation. And as expected, when Luke explains his plans to start his own IT firm, the boss berates him and reminds him how hard it is to start a business and that statistically he will likely fail. The boss gave the final blow as Luke walked out the door: "Luke, you're not that talented. So, when you fail, don't come crawling back here looking for your old job. I'll have you replaced with someone more capable an hour after you turn in your access badge."

Needless to say, Luke had the Mental Toughness to ignore the mean-spirited comments of his jerk boss. If nothing else, this past year taught him that his self-worth doesn't come from his boss' opinion.

Luke had already incorporated his LLC by the time he finished his last two weeks of work. Within a month he had finished coding the timecard application (app) that he previously mentioned to his jerk boss. A month later, he sold a contract for his app and some IT support to an up-and-coming cyber coin company. A year later, he sold the entire business for $10 million dollars.

If Luke would have listened to his jerk boss and all of his negativity, he would still be grinding away nine to five at his miserable old job. Now he is a multimillionaire working on his second tech business.

Self-defense

I need to admit that I was a childhood victim of bullying at public school ... for about fifteen seconds. And then I punched the bully in the face, breaking his nose and knocking him down.

Even back then, my natural disposition was to be nice to everyone and to avoid conflict. But my father had always taught that (1) "no one bullies a Littlestone" and that (2) "most things aren't worth fighting for ... but some are." So, when the bully turned his attention on me, he made a bad mistake.

I'm not a proponent for fighting. But I am a huge proponent of self-defense and Mental Toughness, and I believe that they go hand in hand. If a young kid has the Courage to spar with a larger kid or an adult as part of their jujitsu or karate training, then they are much more physically and mentally prepared to stand up to the bully or to defend themselves from an assaulter or rapist.

Physically tough kids are mentally tough kids. This is why I recommend martial arts or self-defense training for everyone.

It is essential that parents take Responsibility for bestowing and developing Mental Toughness within their children. We now live in a world where "likes" and "followers" are the most desired commodities, and bullies attack you physically and on social media. If your child doesn't have a strong sense of self and resilient Mental Toughness, they are going to get trampled.

Survivor Dad

My favorite survivor instructor at the infamous Survival Evasion Resistance and Escape (SERE) school at Camp Mackall, North Carolina was a Special Forces Master Sergeant who was married and had two kids. He told our group that he likes to take his family camping, and that he teaches them all of the survival techniques that he was teaching us. He went on to tell us that over the summer he dropped off his two kids in the forest on Friday after school and came back to the same spot on Sunday afternoon to pick them up. Besides what they were wearing, he let them have Gortex jackets, a first aid kit, a CB radio for emergency use only, a metal canteen cup, some 550 cord, and two pocket knives. When he picked them up on Sunday, they showed him the camp that they built, the fire they started, and the fish they caught.

I was shocked. But also impressed.

"You see," continued the instructor, "I don't want my kids to be wimps. Too many kids these days are weak, spoiled, ungrateful, unable. Surviving in the woods for two nights when the weather is perfect isn't the hardest thing in the world ... but it is a step in the right direction. And shame on me for not teaching them what I know. It's a hard world out there, and it is only getting worse. I want my kids, and especially my daughter, to be physically and mentally tough. To be ready."

Individual Training / Development Plan: (PTREXAR)

Now is the point where you need to take a break from this book, sit down with a piece of paper, and make a plan on how you are going to train / develop the mindset of Mental Toughness. Use the below questions to help you make your plan.

If you are going to skip this section, then please at least answer the first question: Where am I the least mentally tough?

<u>Plan</u>:
- Where am I the least mentally tough?

- How can I improve my Mental Toughness in that area?
- List three things I can do to increase my Mental Toughness:
    - #1:
    - #2:
    - #3:
- How do I plan to accomplish each of the above?
    - Training Tasks / Behaviors / Actions?
    - Frequency of Training?
    - Milestones / Phases?
- How or where or in what situations can I rehearse showing or displaying Mental Toughness?
- What is the purpose of developing Mental Toughness?
- What is my ultimate Goal / End-State regarding Mental Toughness?
- How can I evaluate if my Mental Toughness training is working?

<u>Train</u>: Go out there and get to work. Start today. Do what you planned (above) to do. Train like you fight. Don't make this easy on yourself. Make your training harder and more difficult, so that when it becomes time to execute your goal, you will be overly prepared.

Rehearse: Put yourself in situations where you will be able to demonstrate Mental Toughness.

Execute: Execute that final display of Mental Toughness for which you have been planning. Accomplish your goal.

Analyze: Assess if your Mental Toughness has grown and developed. Analyze how effective your training plan was. What did you do wrong during this PTREXAR cycle? How can you improve next time?

Repeat: Now get out there and do the whole PTREXAR cycle again! Get even better!

12: Industriousness

Several years ago, I had the honor of being the Commander of all Special Operations Forces in Central America. I was a Company Commander of the best and brightest Green Berets in the Army, augmented by PSYOP and Civil Affairs teams, a couple of airplanes from Airforce Special Operations, and a half dozen SEALs and SWCCs.

Having spent more than twenty-six months forward deployed to Latin America in the war against drugs, I was quite familiar with the threat and the area of operation. My predecessor wasn't lazy, but he was complacent. And since I hate to waste my time and my life, I decided to make as huge of a difference on the war against drugs as possible. I planned what I called Operation CENTURION SUNSET and spent the next five months setting the conditions.

The key to Operation CENTURION SUNSET was that it was going to be a set of simultaneous counter-drug missions in multiple countries against multiple threats. We were going to do only that which we were authorized to do, but at the same time, everywhere we could. I called it centralized leadership but decentralized execution. For example, in country one we were legally authorized to train our partnered counter-drug forces. Nothing more. So, we trained our partnered counter-drug force and set them loose on execution day. In country two, we were allowed to go with our partners into the last covered and concealed location before the objective.

In country three, we were only allowed to share intel and point partners to the location of the bad guys. In country four, we were not allowed to do anything, but other governmental agencies gave thousands of dollars of fuel to maritime harbor police to search and seize ships known to traffic narcotics. I called in every enabler I could think of and got extra money for fueling and feeding our partners. In a fifth country, we couldn't do anything. So I scheduled a huge deception operation ... a helicopter training exercise in a location controlled by the bad guys. The aviators had fun doing a couple days of fast rope training with the locals. But the bad guys panicked. They thought they were under attack and changed their tactics. This disrupted their normal day-to-day operations and caused them to make a few mistakes, upon which we capitalized.

Because of the decentralized nature of the operation, I had nothing to do on the first night of execution. So I slept in, went for a long run and popped into my headquarters after breakfast. Some partnered nations were hugely successful, others only disruptive. Intel was booming.

Over the next week, I watched the fruits of our labor bloom. Friendly forces were gaining momentum, working together for the first time in years. Counter-narcotics units were making raids, seizing drugs, and killing drug traffickers. Drug cartels were in a state of disarray and ended up shutting down operations for over a month. Without violating Operational Security (OPSEC), let's just say that our industrious efforts resulted in millions of dollars of drugs not reaching the USA. We will never know how many lives we saved by preventing so much cocaine from entering the USA.

Definition & Considerations

Industriousness is the noun form of being industrious, defined as "hardworking, diligent, active, busy."[16] Industriousness is one of my all-time favorite traits. It separates the smart from the dumb, the hardworking from the lazy, the proactive from the reactive. I have genuinely found that all SOF are industrious. Members of the Special Operations community are hardworking, deliberate and diligent about what they do and how they train and prepare, always active, and busy making it happen.

---

[16] https://www.collinsdictionary.com/dictionary/english/industrious

Proactive: The industrious person gets out there and makes it happen. They don't sit around and wait for good fortune. Reactive people watch a lot of television and do what their friends recommend. The proactive person makes the news and leads his friends and family where he wants to go.

Hope is not a Method: Industrious people don't hope for success, they make success. In the military we have an expression: "Hope isn't a method." We use this expression during planning, usually when addressing a junior leader who has not yet made an acceptable contingency plan.

"Sir, we hope the weather is going to clear up so we can fly the helicopters to the objective later this evening."

"Hope is not a method, Lieutenant. Go back to your Platoon Sergeant and I'm sure the two of you can come up with a contingency plan for how you are going to get your platoon to the objective if the weather doesn't clear up. Back-brief me in an hour. But no matter what, you and your rifle platoon will be on that hilltop before daybreak."

Figure it Out: Figuring it out is quickly becoming a lost skill these days. Sadly, people are losing their ability to troubleshoot. When faced with a challenge or an obstacle or a problem or bureaucracy, industrious people simply figure it out. Since I retired from the Special Operations community, I have been absolutely surprised how much hand-holding I do. People no longer want to be pointed in the right direction and left to figure it out, which would save everyone time. They want you to hold their hand, like Mommy, and walk them through the process. And by "walking them through the process," I mean you do it for them while they sit there like helpless little children.

<u>No Excuses:</u> Industrious people don't make excuses. They don't blame others. They don't complain endlessly about the situation. They gather the facts and take a wholistic look at the situation, and then they figure it out. They don't blame and complain. Industrious people are all about actions, not excuses.

<u>Make it Happen / Mission Accomplishment:</u> Industrious people make it happen. They simply do the work and get it done. Whether we are talking about a huge project or a small one, industrious people find a way to accomplish their mission.

Could you imagine back-briefing the President: "Sir, we can't go after the number-one terrorist in the world because he is in a large military compound guarded by a dozen bodyguards with machine guns." Of course not. That would be ridiculous. The industrious Special Operations team will make it happen.

To see where each bad guy is, the Special Operations team will fly an unmanned arial vehicle (UAV) over the objective. To mitigate the threat of being observed, the Special Operations team will employ snipers to eliminate the tower guards who will see the helicopters coming. To mitigate the guard force at the compound, the Special Operations team will use smoke to obscure the helicopters and assault force from view. The Special Operators will raid under the cover of darkness using infrared lights and night-vision devices. A violent and well-trained supporting effort will set up an outer ring of security which prevents anyone from leaving the objective compound and destroys any bad guys trying to reinforce the objective compound. Someone will likely get hurt or shot or worse. So expert medics, cross-trained in advance trauma, are integrated into the assault force. Close air support is overhead.

Industrious people, even in the face of enormous challenges, will find a way to make it happen and accomplish their mission.

Take the Initiative: Unlike the couch potato who sits in front of the television all day, the industrious person takes the initiative. You can't get it done unless you are moving. Yes, it is important to think it through and to make a good plan. But it is about action and effort, plus proper time management. You can't accomplish if you aren't busy getting it done.

Network: Because no one is an expert at everything, I have found that industrious people have networks. Even where I am living right now in Italy, I have a tire guy, a dent repair guy, a weapons guy, a tax guy, a buy-a-car guy, an electrician, some doctors, and a few restaurants that will always give me a table even if I don't have reservations. For work, I have my go-to guys, my "help me edit a video" guy, my technological advisor, my social media advisor, my book editor. I want to highlight that all of the members of my network are honorable and accomplished business owners who have earned the right to remain on my rolodex. I could function without them. But my life is much more efficient with them. I recommend that you start building your network of potential teammates who can help you solve the problems and challenges that are certain to happen.

Nonstop Effort: In urban combat training, we use the expression "seek work." The premise is that there is always something to do. You can pull security on a door or out a window. You can "plus up" your magazine or put a new one into your rifle. You can send a report up to higher headquarters, recheck the map, retake accountability of your team and the rest of the assault force. The point is that surviving urban combat requires constant and never-ending work. There is always something to do, and the industrious person will always be working hard for the good of the group. Likewise, there is always something for you to do to make your home or school or work environment better. And this is where the industrious person works hard to make it happen.

<u>Phases or Milestones:</u> We have used the last few paragraphs to encourage you to be proactive, not reactive; to take the initiative, to figure it out and to make it happen. All of this is about action. But because some missions and projects are very complicated, I feel obligated to remind you of the industry best practice of phasing and setting milestones. You can't accomplish everything at once. But perhaps you can do something productive every day, every time you go to school, every time you turn on your computer. Break up your mission into phases or set milestones along your planned process. Accomplishing a milestone or reaching a new phase is always a good reminder that you can and will be successful as long as you keep the forward progress.

<u>Daily routine:</u> The last consideration under Industriousness that I want you to consider is your daily routine. We all have the same twenty-four hours each day. Even if you have a full-time job and need eight hours of sleep a night, there are still several hours remaining in your day. The lazy person checks out and uses them for watching television and engaging in social media. The industrious person has a second job, learns a language, exercises, volunteers, studies. I recommend that you deliberately plan and allocate time for your important tasks and projects so that they become integrated into your daily routine. Industrious people use their time wisely.

What it is

Industriousness is working hard.

Industriousness is staying active. It is progress. It gets you and the team closer to the goal.

Industriousness is being diligent. It is about putting a lot of care and effort into what you do. It isn't simply going through the motions. It is quality effort made with purpose.

Industriousness is being proactive and taking the initiative to do what needs to be done to accomplish the mission and to make it happen.

What it isn't

Industriousness isn't hoping that something will happen or wishing for a certain outcome.

Industriousness isn't passively waiting for things to occur.

Industriousness isn't letting others control your journey or destination.

Good Busy -vs- Bad Busy

There is a difference between being "good busy" and "bad busy." "Good busy" is doing the right things that help you to make it happen. "Bad busy" is about distraction or keeping occupied.

Employees who work for great leaders are usually given the freedom to be industrious and to take the initiative. They are "good busy" and very productive. Employees who work for bad leaders are micromanaged and told what to do. They usually end up working hard, but on the wrong things. Or as long as they put in their eight hours a day and keep busy, it doesn't matter how productive they are. These people are "bad busy."

Another "bad busy" illustration is when you accept bad advice from people who are not experts. You then spend a lot of time being "bad busy" in the wrong direction. It takes double the effort to get back to where you started and triple the effort to get to the destination.

I often think of conventional military leaders as "bad busy." They are always energetically working on things that are peripheral instead of working on the essentials. Focusing on haircuts, reflective belts on base, paperwork approvals and PowerPoint presentations is not the way to win a war. When you are too busy doing the wrong things, there is never enough time to do that which is crucial.

Industrious people are busy doing the right things, not the wrong ones.

Best Indicators Of

The best indicator of Industriousness is <u>action</u>. If you are motivated to do something, then you will do it. Talk is cheap. Your actions speak louder than words. If you are industrious, you accomplish and do. You make it happen.

Another indicator of Industriousness is <u>accomplishment</u>. If you are busy doing the right things, then you are going to accomplish more than most people, and this will make you stick out and earn accolades and awards. This is why overachievers are exceptionally accomplished. They don't just do one remarkable achievement and then quit. They are driven to always do and succeed.

Too Much or Too Little

Too much Industriousness and you become exhausted. I am borrowing this idea from the chapter on Commitment. If you are always working hard and diligently on everything that you do, then you run the risk of burning yourself out.

Too much Industriousness and you risk being exploited. A supervisor can always see who is industrious and who is lazy. The industrious employee will be given more work to do while the lazy one sits back and enjoys doing the minimum. I recommend that you give 100% to everything you do, but be aware of those who will exploit your diligence for their advantage.

Too little Industriousness and you are average, normal, and go with the flow. If this is you, then I recommend working on finding some Motivation and purpose. It can't be that a person has no passion. Life is too short to be lived without purpose, Motivation, and drive.

Implications

If you are industrious then you will (1) be found reliable and (2) accomplish more.

<u>Reliable</u>: An industrious person is able to make it happen. They do and accomplish what they promise. They are reliable.

<u>Accomplish more</u>: If you are always giving a careful effort (diligence) towards everything that you do, then you are going to be exponentially more successful than the multitudes who simply do the minimums and go through the motions. It shows when you give your best. And this is why industrious people are better employees, inventors, entrepreneurs, teachers, spouses, friends, teammates, and leaders.

How it's Built

<u>You build industriousness by</u> <u>taking the initiative to get it done</u>. You must be proactive, not reactive.

Industriousness is built by <u>figuring it out</u>. You don't always need to ask for help. Sometimes you just need to do what you can to figure it out. Of course, there are times where you need to ask for help. But sometimes you just need to figure it out for yourself. I think the key factors for knowing when you need to ask for help, rather than just figure it out for yourself, are when you might (1) violate safety or (2) waste a large amount of time. If you think it is going to be unsafe to figure it out yourself, then ask for help.

If you think you are going to waste too much time figuring it out for yourself, then ask for a point in the right direction. The key is to not have someone else do it for you or hold your hand through the process. This will not help you develop industriousness.

Another way to build industriousness is by <u>trouble shooting</u>, the skill required to figure it out. Trouble shooting is nothing more than systematically checking on the variables that influence the situation to see if you can identify what needs to be done or what needs to be fixed. Think of this as a version or reverse engineering. Sometimes to progress you need to deconstruct or analyze every variable in play and then figure out how to tweak or exploit or repair or change one of these variables so that you can accomplish your mission.

Industriousness is <u>built by learning</u>. If you can't do something, then learn how to figure it out. Have you ever noticed that lazy people want you to give them a fish so they can eat? An industrious person wants you to teach them how to fish so they can always eat.

The Bulletproof Turret

Let me tell you about a brilliant and industrious man by the name of Shane, a Special Forces

Medic, 18D, assigned to the most aggressive SCUBA team in the Special Forces regiment. Shane and I went through dive school together and were even dive buddies for a few of the more difficult training events. What I liked about Shane was that his Intensity matched his intellect. I'm still convinced to this day that Shane has a photographic memory. Anything told to him once or shown to him once, was locked into the vault of his mind forever. He was a no-nonsense guy who always found a way to make it happen.

Back in the early days of the war on terror, HMMWV assault trucks rarely had body armor, and bulletproof turrets to keep the main gunner safe were unheard of. Shane knew this was going to get his teammates killed, and so he had to do something. Thankfully, Shane knew a guy at the headquarters in Baghdad who was an expert mechanic and a master welder. After a quick discussion, Shane ran back to his team room and collected ten pairs of sunglasses. Everyone on his team had just been issued a pair of these expensive sunglasses, and only the SOF guys had them. Shane gave them to the master mechanic / welder, who immediately distributed them to everyone on his team. They were the first non-SOF soldiers to be wearing these sunglasses, and this "gesture of goodwill" bumped Shane's HMMWVs to the top of the list. A day later, and three of Shane's "gun trucks" had bulletproof turrets on them. The welds weren't perfect, and the spray paint was terrible, but the turrets were strong and dependable.

Let me just say that Shane's vehicles got shot up dozens of times. Almost every member of his team got injured during that deployment. Had Shane not been industrious and traded a few pairs of sunglasses for a few hours of welding and a couple of leftover plates of sheet metal, his teammates would never have returned home alive. Never underestimate the power of an industrious person who is committed to accomplishing his mission and making it happen.

My Life

Although most people would say that I am way too busy, I simply think of it as being industrious. On top of making videos and books for "Life is a Special Operation," I also have a forty-hour-a-week project manager job for a Fortune 500 company and do some consulting on the side. I am back in graduate school earning a Doctorate in Business Administration (DBA) with an emphasis on cybersecurity. I just took up the hobby of archery and am learning Italian. I try to ride my mountain bike whenever possible, and of course, I work out four or five times a week.

The good thing is that I have never been happier in my life than I am right now. Finishing this *Special Operations Mindset* book is going to be a great milestone, but then I need to make the voice recording for the audio book, and the videos for the course. There is always something else for me to do. I don't work at it twenty hours a day. But each day I do as much as I can, as quickly and as diligently as I can, in the hours that I don't have programmed for the more important aspects of life, like being a great husband and father. The industrious person doesn't think of it as too much. They simply think of it as life. And we don't want to waste a second of this precious gift.

Learning Another Language

When I was stationed at Special Operations Command–Europe, I went to the local school to take a German course. The young lady who sat next to me, Kim, was a twenty-two-year-old South Korean citizen who had just married her German husband, whom she met while on vacation skiing in Sweden. Kim was going to school to earn her "B1" language certificate, which would enable her to get a job in the local economy.

I always thought I was a good student, but Kim took being industrious to the next level. She answered every question to every exercise in the workbook. If the answer was a verb, then she also would conjugate it in every tense. If the answer was a noun, she would write it again with the article as a direct or indirect object. She would silently repeat every sentence the professor said and would follow along silently, answering every question asked in class as if she was the only student. I finished the class and was happy to graduate. Kim excelled and immediately enrolled in the next course.

Individual Training Plan: (PTREXAR)

Now is the point where you need to take a break from this book, sit down with a piece of paper, and make a plan on how you are going to train / develop the mindset of Industriousness. Use the below questions to help you make your plan.

If you are going to skip this section, then please at least answer the first question: Where am I the least industrious?

Plan:
- Where am I the least industrious?
- How can I improve my initiative in that area?
- List three things I can do to increase my Industriousness:
    - #1:

- - #2:
    - #3:
- How do I plan to accomplish each of the above?
    - Training Tasks / Behaviors / Actions?
    - Frequency of Training?
    - Milestones / Phases?
- How or where or in what situations can I rehearse showing or displaying Industriousness?
- What is the purpose of being industrious?
- What is my ultimate Goal / End-State regarding Industriousness?
- How can I evaluate if my Industriousness training is working?

<u>Train</u>: Go out there and get to work. Start today. Do what you planned (above) to do. Train like you fight. Don't make this easy on yourself. Make your training harder and more difficult, so that when it becomes time to execute your goal, you will be overly prepared.

<u>Rehearse</u>: Put yourself in situations where you will be able to show Industriousness.

Execute: Execute that final display of Industriousness for which you have been planning. Accomplish your goal.

Analyze: Assess if your Industriousness has grown and developed. Analyze how effective your training plan was. What did you do wrong during this PTREXAR cycle? How can you improve next time?

Repeat: Now get out there and do the whole PTREXAR cycle again! Get even better!

13: Readiness

Let me introduce Readiness by talking about a friend of mine from the university whose profession is all about being ready.

It's wretchedly cold and nasty outside as Air Force Captain Johnny Mac comes in from rucking the six-mile perimeter around Bagram Airfield, Afghanistan. He drops his fifty-pound training backpack on to the ground just inside the door of the hangar, which houses his team and their twenty-four-hour operations center. Johnny is glad that the thin metal walls protect the team from the sideways-blowing snow, but he still notices how miserably cold it is inside.

"Anything happen while I was gone?" he asks in his ridiculously slow southern Virginia accent.

Johnny is a Combat Rescue Officer and the leader of a group of Air Force Pararescuemen or "PJs" who are tasked with rescuing downed pilots and providing emergency assistance throughout all of Afghanistan. Like firemen, they train hard but wait around in a constant state of Readiness for a call that they hope will never come. But when it does come, they are out the door within minutes, anxious and absolutely ready to get to their new place of work by land, sea, or air.

"Not much is going on tonight, sir. The weather is crap. Huge storms everywhere. There is a large firefight in the mountains in the northeast; a mounted Infantry company is taking fire along a hillside road in steep terrain. No friendlies killed, but three wounded. A Medevac bird is enroute. Otherwise tonight is pretty quiet."

Johnny strips off a layer of clothes, makes his way to the team refrigerator and pulls out a plate of chocolate chip cookies and the protein shake he prepared before his workout. As soon as he takes his first sip, the radios come alive with chatter.

The Medevac helicopter just crashed. The initial report is that the Taliban shot it down as they came in to evacuate the wounded soldiers. There are survivors, but they are a few hundred meters below the road, at the bottom of the valley.

"Alright guys," John announces to the PJs. "Our bird is the only one with a winch and the power to endure this terrible storm. You know it's coming. I give them a minute before our phone rings. 'A' team, load your gear into the truck. 'B' team, pull up some imagery of the crash site. I want to see what we are getting into."

Johnny walks over to his makeshift desk, kicks off his shoes, and puts on some dry wool socks.

The SIPR (Secret Internet Protocol Router) phone rings. Johnny hits the speakerphone button and finishes tying his boots.

"… this is Arch Angel 6. What's the word?"

Their higher headquarters updates them on the situation. Johnny listens intently, while also observing his men grabbing the extra ropes, maps of the crash site, and the extreme cold-weather gear.

By the time that Johnny hangs up the phone, 'A' team is in full kit and all their team gear is loaded into the back of their F250 Super Duty, ready to deliver their team gear to the Special Operations helicopter that is spinning up a few hundred meters down the runway.

Before Johnny steps out of the hangar to join his team in the dark and snowy night, he gives one last order: "You knuckleheads know I got those cookies from my wife today in a care package. So please, save me at least one."

With that, he shuts the hangar door and heads off to work.

Definition & Considerations

SOF guys refuse to be victims. And this is why they are always prepared for anything. They are always mindful of what could go wrong and how they can prepare for it. They are always physically and mentally ready.

Readiness is defined as "a state of preparation."[17] But prepared for what? I say, prepared for everything.

Let me break down preparation into three subcategories:
1. Physical Readiness
2. Risk Readiness
3. Security Readiness

Let's start with fitness. All SOF are in great shape. This is because physical Readiness and fitness are a part of the Special Operations lifestyle. You will never see a fat Special Reconnaissance Airman. You will never see a MARSOC Raider who can't pass his fitness test. Fitness is "the state of being physically healthy and strong" and "the state of being suitable or good enough for something."[18] Here we can see

---

[17] https://www.merriam-webster.com/dictionary/Readiness
[18] https://www.oxfordlearnersdictionaries.com/definition/american_english/fitness

the two aspects of fitness: (1) health and strength, (2) being suitable and good enough.

<u>Health & Strength</u>: Healthy is the new wealthy. In a world where we can eat food that is laced with chemicals, breath air full of nano-particulates of plastics, and drink our daily calorie requirements in ten minutes, it is increasingly more important to do everything we can to nurture and care for our bodies.

<u>Suitable & Good Enough</u>: Are you fit for duty? Hope so. We don't frequently associate fitness with its sub-definition, suitable and good enough, as in "<u>fit for duty</u>." But one huge aspect of fitness is being capable, prepared, and able to do your duty. And so, I want to add this aspect of fitness to our definition.

<u>Eat like a champion, perform like a champion</u>: Although having a nutritious diet of real and healthy food is an important aspect of maintaining fitness, I have observed that many Special Operators are in amazing physical shape in spite of their diet, not because of it. This certainly was me for many years. I was in great shape, but lived off of protein shakes, Mexican food, and my daily 1,000-calorie Frappuccino from Starbucks. I was a sugar addict who logged many physical accomplishments in spite of my nutrition, not because of it. I don't think this is the right platform

to evangelize a proper diet. But for sure I have learned my lessons and wish I would have practice "cleaner" eating habits two decades ago. I know SOF guys who smoke a cigarette and then run a six-minute mile. I know men who live off of Red Bull or coffee. I know elite athletes in SOF who eat fast food every day for lunch. Although these men are the exception, like all Special Operators, they are elite athletes.

Let's move on to risk Readiness and management. Risk management is all about <u>identifying risk</u> (dangers or things that could go wrong) and then <u>finding ways to mitigate these risks</u>. The military has a painfully bureaucratic mechanism for doing risk management, which involves a lot of paperwork and getting senior officers to approve the residual risk. But paperwork aside, the guys on the ground know from experience what can go wrong, and so it is always in their best interest to find ways to mitigate these risks.

The leading cause of death is cardiovascular disease. SOF guys mitigate this risk by staying in shape. The next leading cause of death is being in a car accident. So, they mitigate these risks by driving a big truck or SUV. It is unlikely that they will be the victim of a terrorist attack at home in the USA, but it is likely that they may be attacked by thieves. So, they carry a pistol or knife and make good decisions about where to go and when. Risk management is about seeing the calamity coming, and then preparing for it in advance. Do you have snow chains in the trunk of your car? Why not? Do you have a first aid kit, extra food and water, a blanket, a weapon, a flashlight? <u>Planning for potential risks and dangers is the best way to be prepared for the worst</u>.

The next aspect of Readiness that I want to address is security. <u>Security is rule # 1</u>. We learn this in Ranger school. We learn this in small unit tactics. We learn this in life. Every single Special Operator I've ever met is a security freak. Bar none.

SOF guys mind their own business. They are quiet professionals who don't talk about their private lives and never discuss anything personal with strangers. Their computers are virus protected, firewalled, and double authenticated. Their houses are fortresses. They drive big cars.

Many SOF guys conceal-carry a pistol everywhere they go. They have a knife in their pocket at all times. They have a weapon in their automobile, and for sure they have an arsenal at home. They aren't irrational about threats, but they know what the threats are and take the appropriate measures to stay safe and secure. They are ready at all times to confront an enemy, or challenge, or accident, or tragedy. They are <u>prepared for the worst</u>.

Security Readiness has many facets. To oversimplify, we have cybersecurity, physical security, information security, and operational security. Cybersecurity protects our computers, smartphones, and devices (cameras, smart houses, etc.) that are attached to the internet from being hacked, destroyed, manipulated, stolen, or sabotaged. Physical security measures protect the infrastructure of where we live and work. Information security safeguards our valuable private information and ideas. And operational security prevents our adversaries from knowing about our important activities and missions. We aren't going to address all of the best practices and behaviors of Special Operations Security in this chapter. But it must be said that security is so integrated into the way a Special Operator thinks that you will likely never find a SOF guy unprepared for the most common threats.

I would like to end the section on Readiness considerations by mentioning <u>contingency planning</u>. A contingency plan in Special Operations is where you deliberately identify everything that could go wrong on the mission and then you plan what to do if any of these contingencies happen. What will we do if the helicopter crashes, or breaks? What if a team member gets shot? What if the radios don't work from inside the objective building? What if the bad guys call in reinforcements? What if the HMMWV breaks down? Think of it as the "what if game." If you plan for all of the "what ifs" that could happen, you will more likely be prepared to deal with contingencies.

What it is

<u>Readiness is being fit enough</u> to conquer what life throws at you. SOF work out five days a week, at a minimum, as a literal requirement of their job. Working out isn't a hobby. It is a lifestyle. They don't just show up at the gym and sandbag. They work out in the rain, the snow, the heat. And they crush every workout. Most SOF have athletic hobbies that they participate in during the weekend. They hike, mountain bike, hunt, cross-train, swim, and do martial arts. They maintain their Readiness and strength 365 days a year.

Readiness is <u>having the appropriate level of strength and endurance to defeat the threat</u>: I like the word appropriate. It conveys that something was thought out and deliberate. The appropriate level of strength and endurance varies between different organizations, missions, and enemy threats. On the bell curve of physical fitness, all

SOF are elite athletes, but only a relative few are the 1% extremes on each side that are either ultra-marathon runners or massive powerlifters. They are appropriately fit to do their mission and counter their threat. For example, you need to be able to ruck all day long with little food to pass Ranger school. The tall, skinny kids have it easier than the beefcakes. The Special Forces Q Course favors the guy with a lot of strength. A Mountain team needs guys who can hike and climb all day. A Direct Action (DA) team needs guys who can fireman's carry another assaulter in full kit (body armor and helmet). A HALO guy doesn't need to have world-class VO2. Gravity does the work to deliver their gear to the landing zone. And dive teams have to swim in all their SCUBA and combat gear. In all these situations, SOF train towards their designated mission set and ensure that they are fit for duty.

Readiness is <u>being preparing for potential or imminent risks and dangers</u>. Whether driving down the highway in Colorado or bounding along a dirt road in northern Iraq, you must always be prepared for the dangers you have identified. If you plan and prepare for the worst, you will always be ready.

Readiness is about always <u>maintaining security</u>. Know the threats in your environment. Maintain situational awareness. Pay attention to your surroundings. Protect yourself and those you love. Make good decisions about where and when to go.

What it isn't

<u>Readiness is not a fad</u>. It isn't popular or in style one month but not another. It is a way of life. Think Boy Scouts: "Be Prepared."

<u>Readiness is not a resolution</u>. This applies mainly to the physical fitness aspect of Readiness. It is very popular these days to make and have New Year's resolutions. But the Truth is, most people don't have the Commitment and Discipline to accomplish their resolution. Rather than simply talking about getting physically fit, let your actions speak louder than your words. Join a gym. Start a fitness program. Work out five days a week, fifty-two weeks a year. Make fitness a lifestyle, not a resolution.

<u>Readiness is never finished</u>. In the Army, you are never done making your fighting position. Although you might have spent all night digging in a textbook-perfect "fox hole," the rule is that you must continuously improve it. Make sure that the overhead cover is reinforced. Clear fields of fire. Validate your range card. Dig grenade sumps …

There is always something else you can do to improve your fighting position. Similarly, you will never reach absolute Readiness. You might think you are prepared, but the supplies in your first aid kit are expired. When was the last time you updated your antivirus, serviced the brakes on your truck, checked the zero on your rifle scope, ran 400 meters as fast as you can? There is always something you can do to be more prepared for what is to come.

Best Indicators Of

The best indicator of physical fitness Readiness is that you are able to take whatever life throws at you. If you neighbor is moving, you can help him move. You are strong enough to put in eight hours lifting and moving furniture. If there is a tragedy and you need to drive through the night to get home to family, you have the physical and mental strength to get to your destination safely. If you are in an emergency situation, you are ready to scale a wall to escape danger or to jump up and out of the way of an oncoming car. If you are physically ready, then you can wear and fight in your body armor all day long.

Another indicator of physical fitness Readiness is better sleep. Couch potatoes and marathon TV watchers always have a problem sleeping. But if you "bring it" every day at the gym, track, or in the pool, then you are likely to be exhausted at the end of the day and to fall asleep sooner and sleep better.

Another indicator of physical fitness Readiness is a higher quality of life. It is heavy to carry around an extra twenty to one hundred pounds of body fat. There are things that you can't do and places you can't go if you are out of shape. A weak person is exhausted after an hour of walking around the Louvre museum and goes to the café for a snack. A fit person can spend eight hours on their feet and is able to enjoy seeing everything the Louvre has to offer. Fit people weigh less, are physically healthier, have less inflammation, are able to do and accomplish more, and live longer.

An indicator of risk Readiness is that you own an appropriate amount of safety and survival gear. I have a scooter helmet, mountain-bike helmet, ballistic helmet, open-face motorcycle helmet, full-face motorcycle helmet, and a snowboard helmet. I value my brain and will take any precaution possible to prevent me from injuring myself. Do you have a first aid kit, tool kits, jumper cables, weapons, a big/safe automobile? People who are prepared for worst-case scenarios usually own tools to ensure their safety and protection.

An indicator of security Readiness is that you only trust a few people, or no one at all. This means you keep your business to yourself and watch what you post on social media. This means you are prepared for robbers, thieves, hackers, pedophiles, terrorists. I'm not implying that SOF guys don't trust anyone. For sure, they trust the men on their left and right, members of their tribe. But everyone else is suspect.

Too Much or Too Little

Too much fitness, and you are weird. Think of the 300-pound steroid junkie in a mini-speedo and a spray tan flexing on stage for their judge's subjective evaluations. Imagine the sad soccer mom who is convinced that her husband thinks she is too fat. She does three or four hours of cardio every day to stay skinny. She looks like a prisoner of war.

Too little fitness, and you are unhealthy. This is most people in Westernized, rich cultures. This lack of fitness leads to inflammation, obesity, laziness, and being unprepared for the emergencies that life sends.

Too much risk management, and you become a safety nerd. No one likes the safety nerd who is best friends with the fun police. Better to be smart about mitigating risk, but still get out there and enjoy life.

Too little risk Readiness, and you are careless. No one likes a careless teammate. He will get you killed.

Too much security Readiness, and you will be paranoid. Make no mistake about it, there are threats out there. Just ask your nearest policeman, paramedic, or soldier. But just because these threats are real, doesn't mean that they are everywhere and that you will become a victim of them. I always recommend being "appropriately paranoid" and taking the right security precautions for any given situation.

Too little security Readiness, and you will eventually become a victim.

Implications Of

If you are ready, then you are going to (1) accomplish more, and (2) have a safer, happier life with (3) more peace.

<u>Accomplish More:</u> Most overweight people are lazy. They make the easy decisions instead of the harder ones that require Discipline or Commitment. I've noticed that healthy and fit people are able to do more in a day than unhealthy people.

And I've seen time and time again that those who are in great shape are able to do anything they set their minds to do.

As far as risk and security Readiness go, those who mitigate risk and are prepared for the worst <u>live to play another day</u>. They saw the calamity coming and prepared for it. They weathered the storm and are now preparing for the next event, not spending the rest of their lives doing consequence management.

<u>Safer Life</u>: If you mitigate risks and take all of the security precautions you can to protect yourself and those you love from harm, then you are going to be much safer than someone who hasn't.

<u>Happier Life</u>: All things being equal, the person who is fit has a happier life than someone who is unfit and unhealthy. Imagine that you are fifty pounds overweight. It takes effort to tie your shoes. It takes effort to walk the stairs to get to your office. It takes more effort to get in and out of the car. You won't have the endurance to waterski, snowboard, mountain bike, or hike. You won't have the endurance to go dancing or have a shopping day where you are on your feet for eight hours and 10,000 steps. You heart works extra hard just to do things that fit people take for granted.

<u>Peace</u>: Being prepared for tough times brings peace. If you aren't prepared for the future, you are more likely to worry about it. If you are prepared for the future, then you don't worry about it.

How It's Built

Physical Readiness is built through working out. There are millions of fitness options available for you to choose from: weights, cardio, calisthenics, ruck marching, martial arts, cross training, sports … And then there are a million other variations for these fitness options: with high weights – low reps, low weight – high reps, free weights, machines, no weights, bands, high-intensity training, circuits, inside, outside, time of the day, duration, fasted, with food … The key is that you don't just accidentally get fit. It is a process, and it requires working out.

Dedicating Time: You can't be lackadaisical about fitness. It has to be a planned priority for your weekly schedule. Whether you are an Air Force TACP who does physical training (PT) with his team for two hours every morning, five days a week, or you are a college student trying to finish your last year of school, everyone who wants to be fit must deliberately plan and execute their fitness program.

Fitness is more successful if it is accompanied with healthy eating. To be honest, and to follow the math, nutrition is more important than working out when it comes to body composition and weight loss. You can do high-intensity training for two hours and burn 1000 calories. Or you can drink a Frappuccino and consume 1,000 sugar calories in fifteen minutes. Making good nutritional decisions is an important way to take your fitness to the next level.

Risk Readiness is built by planning ahead. You have to take a minute to (1) identify what the risks are. And then for each of the risks that you identify, you need to (2) plan a way to mitigate that risk. Once you do it enough, it becomes second nature.

Security Readiness is built by implementing precautions and changing behavior. We all know that cybersecurity threats are real, yet most people quickly accept the terms of service of that newest fad app that is so fun to use on social media. They never realize that that app was coded by a Chinese company, paid for by the Chinese government, and that it tracks your name, contacts, face, location and keystrokes. The security-minded person reads about the new app and then makes an informed decision to download it or not. Most of us know that while crime is a very likely threat, an active shooter is a much more dangerous scenario. But how many of you have discussed what to do in the case of an insider threat with the entire family? Do you establish emergency meeting points whenever you go into a crowded place? Do you make a "no communication plan" in case a cellphone battery goes empty? The point is that you and your loved ones need to be ready for worst-case scenarios. This means you need to talk about worst-case scenarios, have a plan for worst-case scenarios, and even rehearse what you will do during worst-case scenarios.

The Not-So-Crazy Father

Captain Max, his wife and their two teenage daughters were enjoying the opportunity to live and work out of Vicenza, Italy. For New Year's, they decide to go snowboarding in Austria. They plan their route from their house to the ski resort, and it requires them to take the beautiful but infamous "Brenner Pass" through the southern Alps. An experienced and well-trained Special Forces Officer, Max checks Google maps and the weather. They are leaving Friday afternoon, the drive should be four hours, and the weather looks cold but clear. There is a storm expected to pass through Austria early the next morning, and if everything goes well, they will wake up to fresh powder on the slopes. Despite their SUV being extra tight with luggage and snowboards, Max insists that he keep his "car bag" in the vehicle, and he even goes so far as to bring a couple extra blankets and some extra water.

Just north of Bolzano, the weather takes a turn for the worse and it begins to snow. By the time he hits Brixen, Max decides to pull over to put on snow chains. A few kilometers south of the Austrian border, a car slips in the snow and causes a five-car accident just a few meters in front of Max and his family. Max immediately jumps out of the vehicle and sets up his blinking triangle about 100 meters down the road to make sure that no one rear-ends his family. He then checks in with the occupants of the crashed cars. They are all okay, but a commercial truck is sideways in the street and passage is not possible.

As they wait for the authorities to arrive, the snow keeps on coming. By the time the paramedics arrive, it is a foot deep. The ambulance driver reports that there are two other accidents just south of their location, and that it is likely going to be several hours before a snow plow and tow truck arrive to get out the semi-truck and clear a way through.

Max and his family end up spending the night in their vehicle. And when the wrecker and snow plow arrived the next morning, Max had just finished making some hot coffee for the adults and some hot chocolate for the kids.

When asked about it, Max smiled. "For sure I've slept in worse places. But it was especially good for my kids to see that a little preparation goes a long way. No one likes sleeping in a car, but the blankets and ski clothes ensured we were warm, our snacks kept us happy, water kept us hydrated, and my camp stove was a gamechanger because hot chocolate and coffee was a big hit. I couldn't have paid for better family time."

The Hacked Business

A business is too busy making money to invest time and energy into creating an effective cybersecurity policy or employee training plan. One day an employee gets a lucrative offer in a phishing email. The employee clicks on the link and within seconds, a few bites of computer code are let loose into the network. Within forty-eight hours, the hacker has stolen all of the company's proprietary information and intellectual property. He releases a virus, which takes the company a week to unsort, and when they finally get back to normal, their competition releases a new product which takes the market by storm.

Had the company been prepared for a cyberattack, they would not have been the victim of corporate espionage. Had the company been prepared with a proactive cybersecurity policy and employee training program, the spyware would never have penetrated their network.

It is essential that businesses, families, teams, and individuals alike are ready for potential threats. Readiness comes from preparation, not from being a victim and crisis management.

Prepared for a Pandemic

No one anticipates it happening to them. But it could. And for this reason, it is important to be prepared. Whether it is a fire extinguisher in the kitchen, snow chains in the car, or an extra stockpile of food and supplies as you wait out the next pandemic, we can all upgrade our Readiness by planning ahead and purchasing a few extra pieces of safety or survivability gear.

I am writing this book right now during the second wave of the worldwide COVID pandemic. If there is one redeeming thing about this entire pandemic, it is the fact that we have all learned a thing or two about Readiness and preparation. Those who were prepared flourished, while those who weren't suffered. By the time the second wave hit where we are temporarily living, we had a bit more on the shelves and in the pantry, more home fitness gear, a faster internet package, a few more weapons, a new freezer chest in the garage, and new cushions for the porch swing so my wife and I can enjoy the fresh air together. I hope and pray that the second wave of COVID ends soon. But either way, we are flourishing and prepared for the long haul. Planning ahead and being ready always brings more peace.

Individual Training / Development Plan: (PTREXAR)

Now is the point where you need to take a break from this book, sit down with a piece of paper, and make a plan on how you are going to train / develop the mindset of Readiness. Use the below questions to help you make your plan.

If you are going to skip this section, then please at least answer the first question: Where am I the least ready?

Plan:
- Where am I the least ready?
- How can I improve my Readiness in that area?
- List three things I can do to increase my physical Readiness:
    - #1:

- o # 2:
- o # 3:
- List three things I can do to increase my risk Readiness:
    - o # 1:
    - o # 2:
    - o # 3:
- List three things I can do to increase my security Readiness:
    - o # 1:
    - o # 2:
    - o # 3:
- How do I plan to accomplish each of the above?
    - o Training Tasks / Behaviors / Actions?
    - o Frequency of Training?
    - o Milestones / Phases?
- How or where or in what situations can I rehearse showing or displaying Readiness?
- What is the purpose of developing Readiness?
- What is my ultimate Goal / End-State regarding Readiness?
- How can I evaluate if my Readiness training is working?

Train: Go out there and get to work. Start today. Do what you planned (above) to do. Train like you fight. Don't make this easy on yourself. Make your training harder and more difficult, so that when it becomes time to execute your goal, you will be overly prepared.

Rehearse: Put yourself in situations where you will be able to demonstrate Readiness.

Execute: Execute that final display of Readiness for which you have been planning. Accomplish your goal.

Analyze: Assess if your Readiness has grown and developed. Analyze how effective your training plan was. What did you do wrong during this PTREXAR cycle? How can you improve next time?

Repeat: Now get out there and do the whole PTREXAR cycle again! Get even better!

Conclusion

The virtues, characteristics and mindsets of this book are not comprehensive. It would be impossible to capture and describe all of the unique characteristics of those within the elite Special Operations community. Nonetheless, these are the mindsets that I have most frequently observed being displayed by the men I most respect.

Special Operations Training model: **PTREXAR**

P: Plan

    T: Train

        R: Rehearse

            EX: Execute

                A: Analyze

                    R: Repeat.

Inherently, all SOF understand the fact that skills and abilities are improvable. This is why we train so hard, and this is why I recommend that you deliberately plan, train, and rehearse ways to develop your skills and mindsets. And once you get an opportunity to put them into action, you should analyze how it went, and then repeat the entire training cycle again.

Truth: It is impossible to become the best of the best, at anything, if you are lying to yourself about your skills and abilities. The Truth hurts, but you must embrace it and use it to evaluate your performance as you improve your skills and abilities.

Competence comes before Confidence. If you want to become a champion, then you need to master the requisite skills and knowledge of your field of expertise.

Confidence: You build Confidence as you do and accomplish hard things. This will develop a legitimate belief in yourself and your abilities. When coupled with humility, Confidence is an essential building block of the charismatic leader.

Discipline allows you to stick to what you started, facilitates self-control, enforces obedience and order, and helps you do the hard right over the easy wrong.

Commitment is having the follow-through to complete what you promised. It is not about having willpower. It is stronger. There is no turning back. All in.

Motivation is knowing your reason or purpose. It enables your willingness to do something. It helps you endure when the going gets tough.

Responsibility is doing your job and dealing with whatever happens. As an adult, your life is your Responsibility. As a leader, everything that happens or fails to happen to your team, company, unit, or family is your Responsibility. Good leaders give praise, but they also take fault.

Courage requires overcoming fears. It is putting your conviction into action.

Intensity is a derivation of passion, strong emotions and opinions, and is shown through action.

Mental Toughness is built through enduring hardships. It often requires confrontation, but for sure ends with resiliency. A true champion is never broken.

Industriousness requires being proactive, diligent, and hardworking. It is about being good busy, not bad busy. Excuses are not allowed. Take the initiative and figure it out. Make it happen.

Readiness is about being proactive, not reactive, and is best illustrated through physical, risk, and security Readiness. It is making the decision to never be a victim and to remain the master of your own fate.

Thanks for investing in yourself by dedicating the time required to read this book. I genuinely hope that you are now more inspired and better prepared to train and develop the mindset you need to accomplish your mission.

It is now time to stop reading about Special Operations mindsets and to adopt and put these virtues into practice. It is time for action. I've given you the tools to think and perform like a champion. The rest is up to you.

Now get there and accomplish your mission … make it happen!

Life is a Special Operation.
Are you Ready for It?

www.ingramcontent.com/pod-product-compliance
Lightning Source LLC
Chambersburg PA
CBHW072000110526
44592CB00012B/1160